Lecture Notes in Computer Science   14207

Founding Editors

Gerhard Goos
Juris Hartmanis

The series Lecture Notes in Computer Science (LNCS), including its subseries Lecture Notes in Artificial Intelligence (LNAI) and Lecture Notes in Bioinformatics (LNBI), has established itself as a medium for the publication of new developments in computer science and information technology research, teaching, and education.

LNCS enjoys close cooperation with the computer science R & D community, the series counts many renowned academics among its volume editors and paper authors, and collaborates with prestigious societies. Its mission is to serve this international community by providing an invaluable service, mainly focused on the publication of conference and workshop proceedings and postproceedings. LNCS commenced publication in 1973.

Xiuqin Pan · Ting Jin · Liang-Jie Zhang
Editors

Cognitive Computing – ICCC 2023

7th International Conference
Held as Part of the Services Conference Federation, SCF 2023
Shenzhen, China, December 17–18, 2023
Proceedings

Springer

Editors
Xiuqin Pan
Minzu University of China
Beijing, China

Ting Jin
Hainan University
Haikou, China

Liang-Jie Zhang 🆔
Shenzhen Entrepreneurship and Innovation
Federation
Shenzhen, China

ISSN 0302-9743   ISSN 1611-3349 (electronic)
Lecture Notes in Computer Science
ISBN 978-3-031-51670-2   ISBN 978-3-031-51671-9 (eBook)
https://doi.org/10.1007/978-3-031-51671-9

Preface

The 2023 International Conference on Cognitive Computing (ICCC) aimed to cover all aspects of Sensing Intelligence (SI) as a Service (SIaaS). Cognitive Computing is a sensing-driven-computing (SDC) scheme that explores and integrates intelligence from all types of senses in various scenarios and solution contexts. It goes well beyond the standard senses of a human being, namely the four major senses (sight, smell, hearing, and taste) located in specific parts of the body, as well as a sense of touch located all over the body.

ICCC 2023 was a member of the Services Conference Federation (SCF). SCF 2023 had the following 10 collocated service-oriented sister conferences: 2023 International Conference on Web Services (ICWS 2023), 2023 International Conference on Cloud Computing (CLOUD 2023), 2023 International Conference on Services Computing (SCC 2023), 2023 International Congress on Big Data (BigData 2023), 2023 International Conference on AI & Mobile Services (AIMS 2023), 2023 International Conference on Metaverse (METAVERSE 2023), 2023 International Congress on Internet of Things (ICIOT 2023), 2023 International Conference on Cognitive Computing (ICCC 2023), 2023 International Conference on Edge Computing (EDGE 2023), and 2023 International Conference on Blockchain (ICBC 2023).

This volume presents the accepted papers for ICCC 2023. ICCC 2023's major topics included but were not limited to: Cognitive Computing Technologies and Infrastructure, Cognitive Computing Applications, Sensing Intelligence, Cognitive Analysis, Mobile Services, Cognitive Computing on Smart Home, Cognitive Computing on Smart City.

We accepted 9 full papers from 14 submissions. Each was reviewed and selected by three independent members of the ICCC 2023 International Program Committee in a single-blind review process. We are pleased to thank the authors whose submissions and participation made this conference possible. We also want to express our thanks to the Program Committee members, for their dedication in helping to organize the conference and reviewing the submissions. We appreciate your great contributions as volunteers, authors, and conference participants in the fast-growing worldwide services innovations community.

December 2023

Xiuqin Pan
Ting Jin
Liang-Jie Zhang

Organization

General Chair

Ruifeng Xu — Harbin Institute of Technology, China

Program Chairs

Xiuqin Pan — Minzu University of China, China
Ting Jin — Hainan University, China

Services Conference Federation (SCF 2023)

General Chairs

Ali Arsanjani — Google, USA
Wu Chou — Essenlix Corporation, USA

Coordinating Program Chair

Liang-Jie Zhang — Shenzhen Entrepreneurship & Innovation Federation, China

CFO and International Affairs Chair

Min Luo — Georgia Tech, USA

Operation Committee

Jing Zeng — China Gridcom Co., Ltd., China
Yishuang Ning — Tsinghua University, China
Sheng He — Tsinghua University, China

Steering Committee

Calton Pu (Co-chair)	Georgia Tech, USA
Liang-Jie Zhang (Co-chair)	Shenzhen Entrepreneurship & Innovation Federation, China

ICCC 2023 Program Committee

Nagarajan Kandasamy	Drexel University, USA
Supratik Mukhopadhyay	Louisiana State University, USA
Yi Zhou	University of Science and Technology Beijing, China
Liuqing Chen	Zhejiang University, China
Yong Lu	Minzu University of China, China
Dong Wen	University of Science and Technology Beijing, China
Min Lu	Shenzhen University, China
Ye Liu	Institute of Psychology, Chinese Academy of Sciences, China
Peng Xu	Northeast Normal University, China
M. Emre Gürsoy	Koç University, Turkey
Carson Leung	University of Manitoba, Canada
Jing Zeng	China Gridcom Co., Ltd., China
Limin Su	Beijing Union University, China
Dwith Chenna	Magic Leap, USA

Conference Sponsor – Services Society

The Services Society (S2) is a non-profit professional organization that has been created to promote worldwide research and technical collaboration in services innovations among academia and industrial professionals. Its members are volunteers from industry and academia with common interests. S2 is registered in the USA as a "501(c) organization", which means that it is an American tax-exempt nonprofit organization. S2 collaborates with other professional organizations to sponsor or co-sponsor conferences and to promote an effective services curriculum in colleges and universities. S2 initiates and promotes a "Services University" program worldwide to bridge the gap between industrial needs and university instruction.

The Services Sector accounted for 79.5% of the GDP of the USA in 2016. The Services Society has formed 5 Special Interest Groups (SIGs) to support technology- and domain-specific professional activities.

- Special Interest Group on Services Computing (SIG-SC)
- Special Interest Group on Big Data (SIG-BD)
- Special Interest Group on Cloud Computing (SIG-CLOUD)
- Special Interest Group on Artificial Intelligence (SIG-AI)
- Special Interest Group on Metaverse (SIG-Metaverse)

About the Services Conference Federation (SCF)

As the founding member of the Services Conference Federation (SCF), the first **International Conference on Web Services (ICWS)** was held in June 2003 in Las Vegas, USA. Meanwhile, the First International Conference on Web Services - Europe 2003 (ICWS-Europe 2003) was held in Germany in October 2003. ICWS-Europe 2003 was an extended event of the 2003 International Conference on Web Services (ICWS 2003) in Europe. In 2004, ICWS-Europe became the European Conference on Web Services (ECOWS), which was held in Erfurt, Germany. Sponsored by the Services Society and Springer, SCF 2018 and SCF 2019 were held successfully in Seattle and San Diego, USA. SCF 2020 and SCF 2021 were held successfully online and in Shenzhen, China. SCF 2022 was held successfully in Hawaii, USA. To celebrate its 21st birthday, SCF 2023 was held on September 23-26, 2023, in Honolulu, Hawaii, USA with Satellite Sessions in Shenzhen, Guangdong, China.

In the past 20 years, the ICWS community has been expanded from Web engineering innovations to scientific research for the whole services industry. The service delivery platforms have been expanded to mobile platforms, Internet of Things, cloud computing, and edge computing. The services ecosystem has gradually been enabled, value added, and intelligence embedded through enabling technologies such as big data, artificial intelligence, and cognitive computing. In the coming years, all transactions with multiple parties involved will be transformed to blockchain.

Based on technology trends and best practices in the field, the Services Conference Federation (SCF) will continue to serve as the umbrella code name for all services-related conferences. SCF 2023 defined the future of New ABCDE (AI, Blockchain, Cloud, Big-Data, & IOT) as we enter the 5G for Services Era. The theme of SCF 2023 was **Metaverse Era.** We are very proud to announce that SCF 2023's 10 co-located theme topic conferences all centered around "services", while each focused on exploring different themes (web-based services, cloud-based services, Big Data-based services, services innovation lifecycle, AI-driven ubiquitous services, blockchain-driven trust service-ecosystems, industry-specific services and applications, and emerging service-oriented technologies).

- Bigger Platform: The 10 collocated conferences (SCF 2023) were sponsored by the Services Society, which is the world-leading not-for-profit organization (501 c(3)) dedicated to the service of more than 30,000 worldwide Services Computing researchers and practitioners. A bigger platform means bigger opportunities for all volunteers, authors, and participants. Meanwhile, Springer provided sponsorship for best paper awards and other professional activities. All the 10 conference proceedings of SCF 2023 were published by Springer and indexed in the ISI Conference Proceedings Citation Index (included in Web of Science), Engineering Index EI (Compendex and Inspec databases), DBLP, Google Scholar, IO-Port, MathSciNet, Scopus, and zbMATH.

- Brighter Future: While celebrating the 2023 version of ICWS, SCF 2023 highlighted the Second International Conference on Metaverse (METAVERSE 2023), which covered immersive services for all vertical industries and area solutions. Its focus was on industry-specific services for digital transformation. This will lead our community members to create their own brighter future.
- Better Model: SCF 2023 will continue to leverage the invented Conference Blockchain Model (CBM) to innovate the organizing practices for all the 10 theme conferences. Senior researchers in the field are welcome to submit proposals to serve as CBM Ambassador for an individual conference to start better interactions during your leadership role in organizing future SCF conferences.

Contents

Research Track

High-Precision Detection of Suicidal Ideation on Social Media Using
Bi-LSTM and BERT Models 3
    Zhenxi Wang, Mingzhe Jin, and Yong Lu

P-Reader: A Clue-Inspired Model for Machine Reading Comprehension 19
    *Jiahao Kang, Liang Yang, Yuefan Sun, Yuan Lin, Shaowu Zhang,
    and Hongfei Lin*

An Unsupervised Method for Sarcasm Detection with Prompts 34
    *Qihui Lin, Chenwei Lou, Bin Liang, Qianlong Wang, Zhiyuan Wen,
    Ruibin Mao, and Ruifeng Xu*

ENER: Named Entity Recognition Model for Ethnic Ancient Books Based
on Entity Boundary Detection 47
    Lifeng Zhao, Ziquan Feng, Na Sun, and Yong Lu

An Enhanced Opposition-Based Golden-Sine Whale Optimization
Algorithm 60
    Yong Lu, Chao Yi, Jiayun Li, and Wentao Li

T4S: Two-Stage Screenplay Synopsis Summary Generation with Turning
Points 75
    *Depei Wang, Wenyi Sun, Cheng Luo, Dachang Liu, Ruibin Mao,
    and Ruifeng Xu*

Application Track

Multi-Factor Water Level Prediction Based on IndRNN-Attention 89
    Haifeng Lv, Yishuang Ning, Ke Ning, Sheng He, and Hongquan Lin

Ethereum Public Opinion Analysis Based on Attention Mechanism 100
    Xianghan Zheng, Wenyan Zhang, Jianxian Zhang, and Weipeng Xie

Prompt Tuning Models on Sentiment-Aware for Explainable
Recommendation 116
    Xiuhua Long and Ting Jin

Author Index 133

Research Track

High-Precision Detection of Suicidal Ideation on Social Media Using Bi-LSTM and BERT Models

Zhenxi Wang[1] ⓘ, Mingzhe Jin[2] ⓘ, and Yong Lu[2](✉) ⓘ

[1] Queen Mary University of London, London 15 2ZL, UK
[2] Minzu University of China, Beijing 100190, China
{21301967,2006153}@muc.edu.cn

Abstract. In a poignant moment on social media, a post suggesting suicidal thoughts is rapidly overshadowed by an array of memes, updates, and ads. Such overlooked cries for help underscore the dire need for reliable detection mechanisms. Addressing this urgent issue, our research introduces an innovative approach to detecting suicidal ideation from text. Using TF-IDF and Chi-square tests, we identify crucial keywords and narrow them down for frequency analysis. Our framework leverages Word2Vec embeddings and is further enriched with readability scores, sentiment assessments via TextBlob, and text length metrics. Latent Dirichlet Allocation (LDA) aids in topic modeling, its insights visualized through compelling word clouds. This multifaceted approach enhances predictive accuracy and provides a nuanced understanding of suicidal ideation. We initially employed conventional algorithms like AdaBoost, Random Forest, XGBoost, and Logistic Regression before transitioning to advanced deep learning models. The Bi-LSTM and BERT models emerged as top performers, achieving detection accuracies of 97% and 98%, respectively. While our study is constrained by dataset limitations and potential biases, it marks a significant step forward in the identification of suicidal tendencies in digital spaces. Looking forward, broader dataset integration, refined models, and a continuous recalibration in line with evolving digital discourse are anticipated next steps.

Keywords: Suicidal Ideation · Machine Learning · Deep Learning

1 Introduction

Suicide stands as a formidable global health crisis, accounting for nearly 800,000 fatalities each year, and emerging as the second leading cause of death among individuals within the age bracket of 15 to 29A comprehensive, multi-pronged strategy is pivotal for efficacious suicide prevention [2]. This strategy encompasses the early detection of suicidal ideation, timely intervention, provision of mental health services, and rigorous research on effective prevention measures. The World Health Organization (WHO) champions structured national strategies for suicide prevention and extends guiding principles for their execution [2, 3].

© The Author(s), under exclusive license to Springer Nature Switzerland AG 2024
X. Pan et al. (Eds.): ICCC 2023, LNCS 14207, pp. 3–18, 2024.
https://doi.org/10.1007/978-3-031-51671-9_1

Traditionally, the detection of suicidal ideation has heavily relied on clinical evaluations and surveys, which, in the digital era, have exhibited limitations due to biases and constraints on real-time monitoring [4, 5]. The advent of social media platforms, now boasting a user base of nearly 4 billion, has emerged as a new arena for individuals to express their thoughts and emotions [17]. Notably, a substantial proportion of these users fall within the age range of 15–29, which coincidentally aligns with the demographic most susceptible to suicide. This digital shift, while presenting an unparalleled opportunity for the early detection of suicidal ideation, also introduces distinct challenges including the management of extensive data, preservation of privacy, and the development of culturally resonant interventions.

We discuss our methodology, the implications of our findings, and the vital role of digital platforms in modern mental health interventions. Through this effort, we highlight the significance of leveraging advanced NLP and ML technologies to address the digital age challenges and opportunities for suicide prevention. Findings, and the critical role of digital platforms in modern mental health interventions.

Contributions of this Paper:

1. Identification and analysis of discriminative keywords more prevalent in texts related to suicidal ideation versus non-suicidal content. This contributes to a focused lexicon valuable for future studies aiming for more accurate text classification in suicide prevention context.
2. Utilization of Latent Dirichlet Allocation (LDA) for theme analysis, which not only identifies prevalent themes in suicidal ideation but also uncovers thematic inertia and interconnections between these themes. This analytical groundwork could guide targeted interventions and prevention strategies by addressing specific aspects of suicidal ideation.
3. Development of specialized feature extraction techniques improving machine learning models' performance on comparable datasets. Notably, our deep learning models achieved high accuracy rates of 97% with Bi-LSTM and 98% with BERT, setting new benchmarks in the field.

The rest of the paper is organized as follows. Section 2 reviews relevant work on the detection of suicidal ideation through social media. Section 3 outlines our methodology, focusing on keyword extraction, topic modeling, and feature selection, along with the models used and evaluation metrics. Section 4 details the experimental setup and procedures. Section 5 is devoted to performance evaluation, result visualization, and analysis. Finally, Sect. 6 offers conclusions, while Sect. 7 suggests potential avenues for future research.

2   Related Work

With the integration of social media data, machine learning, and Natural Language Processing (NLP), significant advancements have been made in the field of mental health monitoring. Early work by Rajesh and Priya laid the groundwork for our research on Reddit by emphasizing the potential of social media platforms like Facebook for identifying symptoms of depression and anxiety [6].

In the realm of NLP, Desmet and Hoste used a binary Support Vector Machine (SVM) to detect 15 different emotions related to suicidal behavior, achieving an F-score of 68.86% [7]. This result validates the feasibility of employing sentiment analysis to discern suicidal intentions. Furthermore, Giachanou and Crestani conducted a comprehensive survey of sentiment analysis methods on Twitter, incorporating various feature extraction algorithms such as TF-IDF, N-grams, and Word2Vec [1]. Oussous et al. highlighted the key role of sentiment analysis in NLP, particularly in mining user opinions on social platforms and blogs [8]. Tadesse et al. also focused on Reddit, employing NLP techniques like TF-IDF and BOW for feature extraction [9]. These works collectively underscore the pivotal role of NLP in our study, where we plan to leverage techniques like TF-IDF, N-grams, and Word2Vec for feature extraction.

Regarding the application of machine learning and deep learning, Braithwaite et al. utilized algorithms such as decision trees and random forests to effectively differentiate between populations at risk of suicide and those who are not [10]. O'Dea et al. further confirmed that machine learning methods could effectively classify suicidal intentions on Twitter [4]. Tadesse et al. achieved an accuracy of 91% in detecting depression-related posts on Reddit using a combination of LIWC, LDA, and bigrams with a Multilayer Perceptron (MLP) classifier [11]. These studies collectively demonstrate the efficacy of machine learning algorithms in tasks related to the classification of suicidal ideation and also suggest that LDA can serve as a feature for classification. We plan not only to use LDA as a classification feature but also to conduct topic analysis on it.

Recent research indicates that deep learning technologies like LSTM and CNN excel in sentiment analysis tasks. For instance, Singh et al. improved the accuracy of sentiment analysis related to suicide by 20% using an LSTM-RNN with attention mechanisms [12]. Aldhyani et al. achieved an astonishing 95% accuracy rate on Reddit using a CNN-BiLSTM model [13]. We intend to use the same public Reddit dataset that they used, as the "SuicideWatch" subreddit has proven to be a reliable data source for analyzing suicidal intentions. Despite its high accuracy, we identified limitations in their study, such as the inclusion of non-discriminative words like "want" and "like" in their word clouds. We aim to focus on identifying truly discriminative keywords and improving model accuracy.

In summary, our work leverages advanced NLP and machine learning techniques to address gaps in feature extraction and model interpretability in current studies. We aim to produce more discriminative word clouds, conduct reliable topic analyses, and offer a comprehensive solution for detecting suicidal intentions on social media.

3 Methodology

3.1 Preprocessing

Text Preprocessing in Traditional Machine Learning. It transforms raw text into a structured format, suitable for algorithmic analysis. Popular libraries like the Natural Language Toolkit (NLTK) are often employed to implement these operations. The core preprocessing techniques are:

Case Normalization: All textual data is standardized to lowercase to eliminate variations attributed to case differences.

Stopword Filtering: Linguistically insignificant words, such as "the" and "a," are removed to enhance the focus on the key content.

Tokenization: Text is divided into basic semantic units, which could be words or phrases, simplifying the subsequent linguistic analysis.

Stemming: Words are stripped down to their root forms to reduce dimensionality.

Bi-LSTM Preprocessing Steps

Text Normalization, Tokenization and Stopword Removal. The same procedures as described above were followed.

Truncation and Padding: Bi-LSTM demands fixed-length sequence inputs. Thus, sequences exceeding predetermined lengths are truncated, while those falling short are padded, typically with zeros.

Sequence Encoding: Words or tokens are mapped to integers or vectors to facilitate numerical computations essential for the gradient-based optimization algorithms.

BERT Preprocessing Steps

Text Normalization: The text is consistently converted to lowercase.

WordPiece Tokenization: BERT uses a unique tokenization method that breaks down words into reusable subwords or characters.

Special Token Insertion: Tokens such as [CLS] and [SEP] are appended to signify the beginning and the end of sentences, respectively.

Truncation and Padding: BERT requires fixed-length inputs, so longer sequences are truncated and shorter ones are padded to meet this length requirement.

Attention Masking: Masks help the attention mechanism focus on relevant content and ignore padding, making computation more efficient.

3.2 Keyword Extraction

In suicide research, accurately identifying keywords related to suicidal tendencies is crucial. Conventional methodologies often employ term frequency-inverse document frequency (TF-IDF) or frequentist approaches to isolate these crucial terms. However, such methods exhibit limitations as they often yield words that, despite their high frequency in suicidal texts, also appear with comparable prevalence in non-suicidal content, thereby lacking discriminative power. To address this shortcoming, we have innovatively combined TF-IDF with Chi-square statistical tests.

Delta TF-IDF: Expanding upon the foundational construct of Term Frequency-Inverse Document Frequency (TF-IDF), our research incorporates a specialized metric known as Delta TF-IDF. While TF-IDF is a well-established measure in information retrieval used to assess the importance of a term within a document, our unique focus requires a more nuanced approach. To distinguish keywords that are particularly relevant to suicidal ideation, we introduce Delta TF-IDF, mathematically defined as:

$$\Delta TF - IDF = TF - IDF_{Suicidal} - TF - IDF_{Non-Suicidal} \tag{1}$$

This enhanced metric enables us to highlight terms that are not only frequent but also uniquely significant within the framework of suicidal texts.

Chi-Square: The Chi-square test is used to check the relationship between a term and its document category. A higher Chi-square value means the term is more closely related to that category.

3.3 Feature Extraction

Word2Vec: This algorithm creates dense vectors for individual words based on their surrounding context, thereby capturing semantic relationships.

PCA (Principal Component Analysis): Used for reducing the dimensionality of high-dimensional data, PCA retains the most significant variables while discarding the less important ones.

LDA: LDA modeling produces topic-based features, like the distribution over topics and dominant topics, to provide richer information for each document.

Readability Score: Readability scores serve as a potential mirror to the writer's cognitive state. Texts produced by disturbed or distracted minds may be either too convoluted or too simplistic.

TextBlob for Sentiment Analysis: Sentiment polarity scores range from -1 (extremely negative) to $+1$ (extremely positive) and measure the text's emotional tone.

Text Length: Number of words in text.

Word Frequency: Number of occurrences of keyword in document.

GloVe Embeddings for Bi-LSTM: GloVe (Global Vectors for Word Representation) is designed to capture both the global statistical information and local semantics of words in a vector space. Given a corpus, GloVe pre-trains word vectors in a way that the dot product of two word vectors is equal to the logarithm of the probability of those words' co-occurrence probabilities.

BERT Embeddings for Bert: We employed the 'bert-base-uncased' variant of the BERT (Bidirectional Encoder Representations from Transformers) model for feature extraction. We specifically extracted the feature vectors, also known as embeddings, from the second-to-last layer of the BERT architecture. And embeddings from this layer optimally capture a balanced combination of both semantic meaning and contextual awareness.

3.4 Models

AdaBoost: We selected AdaBoost for its ability to adapt to complex instances, thereby potentially improving overall model performance.

Random Forest: This model was chosen for its inherent capability to manage high-dimensionality while mitigating the risks of overfitting.

XGBoost: Employed for its proficiency in managing sparse datasets and ensuring rapid, effective modeling.

Logistic Regression: We utilized Logistic Regression to quantify the influence of individual features on the propensity for suicidal behaviors and to compare its performance against more complex models.

K-Nearest Neighbors (KNN): This non-parametric algorithm was selected because of its adaptability to diverse datasets with non-linear feature relationships.

Naive Bayes (NB): We opted for this probabilistic approach based on Bayes' theorem, for its computational efficiency in high-dimensional data and its robustness against irrelevant features.

LightGBM: Utilized for its gradient boosting capabilities and high efficiency.

Bi-LSTM: We employed a Bi-LSTM model for sequence data processing, benefiting from its capacity to address the vanishing gradient problem. Our architecture includes a pretrained embedding layer, followed by a bidirectional LSTM layer with a 50% dropout rate.

BERT: We exploited BERT's capabilities in interpreting text and recognizing nuances, making it particularly suitable for suicide-related text classification. We used the pretrained 'bert-base-uncased' model, fine-tuning it for binary classification. Preprocessing involved using the BERT tokenizer to standardize text lengths.

3.5 Evaluation Metrics

To effectively evaluate the performance of these models, it's essential to first familiarize ourselves with the key evaluation metrics that serve as our benchmarks: Accuracy, Precision, Recall, and F1-Score. Following this, we will go into detail about the specific formulas used to calculate these metrics. Within these formulas, the variables 'TP' (True Positives), 'FP' (False Positives), 'FN' (False Negatives), and 'TN' (True Negatives) play critical roles in determining the values of these key performance indicators.

Accuracy: The ratio of correct predictions to total predictions. Calculated as:

$$accuracy = \frac{TP + TN}{TP + TN + FP + FN} \tag{2}$$

Precision: The ratio of true positives to all positive predictions. Calculated as:

$$precision = \frac{TP}{TP + FP} \tag{3}$$

Recall: The ratio of true positives to all actual positives. Important for minimizing missed cases of suicidal ideation. Calculated as:

$$recall = \frac{TP}{TP + FN} \tag{4}$$

F1-Score: The harmonic mean of precision and recall. Calculated as:

$$F1 = \frac{2 * precision * recall}{Precision + recall} \tag{5}$$

4 Experiments

4.1 Experimental Environment

We conducted our research on Google Colab, leveraging a T4 GPU for computational power. The software environment was standardized with Python version 3.10.12, PyTorch version 2.0.1+cu118, and NLTK version 3.8.1.

4.2 Dataset

In this study, we employed the Kaggle-accessible 'Suicide and Depression Detection' dataset, compiled via the Pushshift API. The dataset comprises 232,074 Reddit posts, dated from December 16, 2008, to January 2, 2021, and sourced from two distinct subreddits: 'SuicideWatch' and 'teenagers.' Posts originating from 'SuicideWatch' were classified as 'suicidal' and served as the primary focus, whereas those from 'teenagers' functioned as the non-suicidal control group. Structurally, the dataset includes two principal columns: 'text,' housing the post content, and 'class,' categorizing each entry as 'suicidal' or 'non-suicidal.' Our dataset features a 1:1 ratio between suicidal and non-suicidal classes, thereby facilitating unbiased model training.

4.3 Preprocessing

Before diving into feature extraction and model training, we first needed to understand and preprocess our dataset. The primary steps undertaken are:

Dataset Split. The dataset was partitioned into training and test subsets using an 8:2 ratio. And we set a fixed random_state of 10.

Text Length Visualization. In text-based machine learning, text length can be a vital clue, hinting at distinct patterns associated with specific labels or outcomes. Analyzing the distribution of these lengths becomes a cornerstone for crafting effective preprocessing strategies. The disparity in text lengths between suicidal and non-suicidal posts is evident in Fig. 1, with suicidal texts generally being more extended.

The histogram in Fig. 2 shows a positively skewed distribution, indicating that some users are elaborating their thoughts in greater detail. For models like BERT and LSTM, we standardized text lengths to improve performance. In contrast, traditional machine learning models used the original text lengths to maintain potential classification cues.

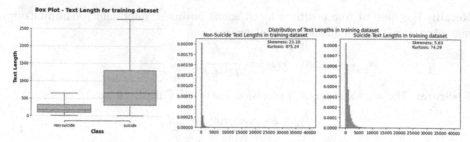

Fig. 1. Box Plot   **Fig. 2.** Positively Skewed Distribution of Text Lengths

Text Preprocessing for Traditional Machine Learning Models. In our quest for the optimal preprocessing strategy, we deployed a Python-based combinatorial approach to systematically examine an array of preprocessing techniques. Utilizing a "chain-like" method, we enabled these techniques to be freely permuted in various combinations, thereby facilitating an exhaustive search for the most effective preprocessing sequence for our model. Following this rigorous analysis, the resultant optimized preprocessing pipeline was distilled into three essential components: Case Normalization, Stopword Filtering, and Tokenization.

Text Preprocessing for Bi-LSTM. Standardized inputs to a fixed sequence length of 50 after normalizing and tokenizing the text.

Text Preprocessing for BERT: Employed specialized tokenization limited to 64 words and used attention masks to focus on meaningful content.

4.4 Keyword Extraction

We aimed to extract the top 100 terms based on delta TF-IDF values. To achieve a clearer distinction, we augmented the stopword list with terms like "like" and "one." Acknowledging the limitations of focusing solely on individual words, we also employed an n-gram model with a range of (2, 4) to capture meaningful phrases. To further refine the feature selection process, we imposed a limit of 5,000 maximum features. Subsequently, we extracted the top 100 terms, which are visualized in a word cloud (**Fig. 3**). Additionally, we conducted a chi-square test on texts related to suicide, identifying another 100 terms that are strongly associated with suicide labels (Fig. 4).

By closely observing Fig. 3 and Fig. 4, we manually selected a set of keywords that are highly indicative of suicidal ideation based on our judgment. Phrases like 'commit suicide,' 'tried kill,' and 'going kill' are direct verbalizations of suicidal intent, underscoring the urgent need for intervention. On the other hand, terms such as 'mental health,' 'getting worse,' 'depression anxiety,' and 'someone talk' serve as subtler markers pointing to deteriorating emotional or mental states that may escalate into suicidal thoughts if not addressed. Here selected keywords will subsequently be utilized as additional features, for which we will calculate word frequency.

Fig. 3. Top 100 keywords TF-IDF Differentiating Suicide and Non-Suicide texts

Fig. 4. Top 100 keywords with highest chi-squared scores

4.5 Feature Extraction

Feature Extraction based on Traditional Machine Learning

Word Frequency. Building upon the keywords previously extracted, we developed a function named "calculate_keyword_frequencies()" to quantify the prevalence of these critical terms within the dataset. This addition furnishes our model with a straightforward yet efficacious dimension, offering a numerical representation of potential suicidal ideation in the text.

Readability Scores. To gain insights into the inherent complexity or simplicity of the textual data, we utilized the textstat library to compute readability scores. Specifically, we employed 'flesch_reading_ease' to provide a score usually ranging between 0 and 100, where lower scores denote more complex texts. Additionally, we used 'smog_index', a numerical estimate where higher values suggest that the text requires advanced comprehension skills. Both of these scores are integrated into our model as separate features, providing a multifaceted view into the text's complexity.

Word2Vec. Using gensim's Word2Vec algorithm, we map each word to a high-dimensional vector to capture its semantic essence. To represent the overall semantic theme of the text, we compute the average of all word vectors. Recognizing that high dimensionality can complicate modeling efforts, we employ Principal Component Analysis (PCA) to reduce the vector dimensions while retaining the most significant information within two principal components.

Sentiment Analysis. We leveraged the TextBlob library to compute a sentiment polarity score for each text, providing a quantitative measure of emotional tone. The model, by factoring in sentiment scores, gains an additional layer of sophistication, potentially identifying a stronger inclination towards suicidal tendencies, which are often deeply interwoven with negative emotions and feelings of despair.

Text Length. Text length is a numeric feature, providing a direct count of characters within a text. Our findings suggest that texts indicating suicidal tendencies tend to be longer than non-suicidal texts.

Topic Modeling (LDA)

Selection of Vectorizer and Model Optimization. Perplexity from both CountVectorizer and TfidfVectorizer were compared. Given the minimize perplexity, TfidfVectorizer was chosen for text transformation. The Latent Dirichlet Allocation (LDA) algorithm was then employed to unearth latent topics. To ascertain optimal parameters, we examined perplexity trends as portrayed in Fig. 5 and Fig. 6. For the TfidfVectorizer, we determined an n-gram range of (1, 3) and capped the maximum features at 5,000 according to minimize perplexity. The LDA parameters were optimized through a grid search, assessing varying numbers of topics, learning methods, and maximum iterations. Using the criterion of minimum perplexity, the most suited parameters were: the "batch" learning method, max_iter set to 30, and n_components as 10.

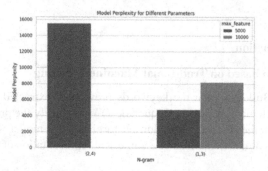

Fig. 5. Perplexity for Different TfidfVectorizer Parameters

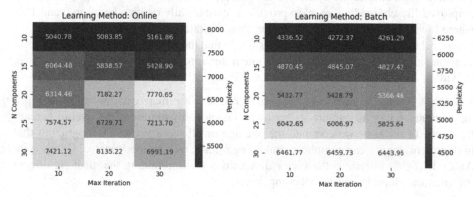

Fig. 6. Comparative Perplexity Analysis Across LDA Parameters

Topic Extraction, Visualization, and Thematic Interpretation. Our topic modeling approach, utilizing the LDA algorithm, identified several themes encapsulating various aspects of life and emotional states that have potential associations with suicidal ideation. To delve deeper into the nuances of each topic, we extracted the top 15 keywords. These keywords were then visually represented through word clouds, as showcased in Fig. 7, offering a lucid depiction of the themes concerning suicidal tendencies. The word clouds serve as an initial touchpoint, but to truly understand their implications, a thematic analysis was essential. This section provides a comprehensive exploration of the identified themes and elaborates on their real-world relevance. The analysis for each theme is as follows:

(a) **Nighttime Lifestyle**: This theme emphasizes the strong association between sleep disorders, like insomnia, and mental health challenges. The chronic lack of sleep can exacerbate feelings of depression, which, in turn, might enhance suicidal tendencies.
(b) **Interpersonal Relationships & Attraction**: This underscores the complexities of human relationships. The struggles of self-worth and romantic challenges can be overwhelming, especially for teenagers who are still forming their identity and self-esteem.
(c) **Education & School Life**: The modern education system, peer dynamics, and pressures of future aspirations can lead to immense stress. Isolation and bullying are notable triggers for depressive thoughts and subsequent suicidal ideation.
(d) **Media Sharing & Online Interactions**: The digital age brings both solace and distress. While online platforms can provide comfort, they can also be a ground for cyberbullying and a trigger for feelings of inadequacy, leading to heightened suicidal risks.
(e) **Societal Views & Politics**: Contemporary societal complexities tied to race, gender, and culture often bring along feelings of alienation. Being constantly judged or pressurized by societal norms can induce feelings of desolation.
(f) **Emotional Outreach & Interaction**: Human beings are social creatures. The lack of meaningful interactions and a supporting network can intensify feelings of loneliness, a known precursor to suicidal tendencies.
(g) **Personal Life & Relationships**: Daily struggles, whether in personal relationships or work-related stress, can take a toll on one's mental health, pushing individuals towards feelings of despair and hopelessness.
(h) **Contemplation of Life & Suicidal Thoughts**: This theme is a poignant reminder of how deeply personal reflections can sometimes lead to overwhelming emotions and, in turn, suicidal ideation.
(i) **Depression and Despair**: This theme needs little explanation, as depression is one of the most significant risk factors for suicide. A culmination of various life experiences and genetic predispositions can lead to this state.
(j) **Everyday Interactions & Events:** This theme underlines that even daily activities, if perceived negatively or stressfully, can elevate suicidal risks, particularly for those on the emotional edge.

The interconnectedness among these themes unveils a intricate psychological ecosystem, where each theme intricately interlaces with others, forming a comprehensive network of influences. For instance, the "Nighttime Lifestyle" theme, with sleep disorders, can directly impact emotional well-being, subsequently manifesting an effect in the "Interpersonal Relationships & Attraction" theme, potentially undermining individual self-esteem. Similarly, challenges from the "Education & School Life" theme, encompassing stress and bullying, along with the virtual challenges of the "Media Sharing & Online Interactions" theme, can intertwine and significantly affect an individual's psychological health. The cyclic relationships among these themes are equally noteworthy. For example, a lack of sleep could lead to emotional issues, which in turn may affect sleep quality, establishing a vicious cycle. By identifying connections across different themes, we are better equipped to provide early intervention and comprehensive support to individuals, thereby reducing the risk of suicide.

Features Derived from LDA Modeling. We introduced topic features, namely from topic_0 to topic_9, derived from Latent Dirichlet Allocation (LDA). These features indicate the degree to which a document associates with each LDA-produced topic. Specifically, the values represent the probability distribution, highlighting the alignment of the document's content with a given topic. The higher the value, the more pronounced is the document's association with that particular topic. Additionally, we defined the 'dominant_topic' feature for every document, pinpointing the topic with the strongest connection compared to others.

Feature Extraction Based on Bi-LSTM. In our research, we opted for the GloVe (Global Vectors for Word Representation) model for word embeddings, prioritizing its capacity to capture both global statistical properties and local semantics of words. This choice forms the cornerstone of our context-rich analysis. Words within the text are transformed into 300-dimensional vectors using these pre-trained GloVe embeddings, which effectively encapsulate semantic relationships between words. This robust representation serves as a foundational input for our Bi-LSTM model, enabling it to perform text classification with nuanced understanding. One of our key discoveries is that the bidirectional context comprehension of Bi-LSTM, when coupled with GloVe embeddings, enhances the model's ability to effectively classify texts and detect subtle changes in context.

Feature Extraction Based on BERT. In our study, we employed BERT (Bidirectional Encoder Representations from Transformers) for its revolutionary bidirectional approach to understanding word context from both preceding and following text. This feature renders BERT exceptionally suited for tasks requiring nuanced interpretation. We utilized the pretrained 'bert-base-uncased' model to transform words or even entire sentences into contextually rich embeddings, thereby ensuring that each word's representation is influenced by its surrounding context. A key contribution of our work lies in leveraging BERT's deep contextual understanding to achieve marked improvements in detecting suicidal ideation within the textual data.

4.6 Training

We split the training set into training and validation subsets. For traditional machine learning models like AdaBoost, Random Forest, and XGBoost, we selected key features using SelectKBest. We fine-tuned hyperparameters using RandomizedSearchCV, which is more efficient than Grid Search for high-dimensional datasets.

Fig. 7. Word Cloud For 10 Topics

For the deep learning models, Bi-LSTM and BERT, we adopted specific training strategies. For Bi-LSTM, we utilized the Adam optimizer, the ReduceLROnPlateau scheduler, and implemented early stopping based on validation loss. For BERT, we employed the AdamW optimizer, a dynamic learning rate scheduler, and early stopping based on validation loss.

Finally, the model that performed best on the validation subset was selected for the final evaluation on an independent test set.

5 Results

5.1 Model Performance

Our model results are displayed in Fig. 8. It's noteworthy that while LightGBM and XgBoost hold their ground with robust metrics above 0.9 in the machine learning landscape, our cutting-edge deep learning models—particularly Bi-LSTM and BERT—elevate the performance standards to 0.97 and 0.98, conclusively highlighting the superior capabilities of deep learning methodologies.

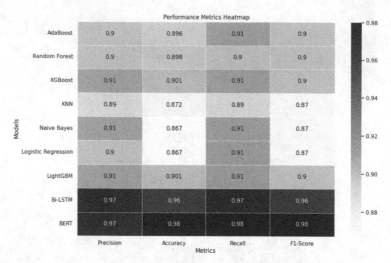

Fig. 8. Performance Metrics Heatmap: Comparing Models for Suicidal Ideation Detection

5.2 Comparative Analysis

We selected NIKHILESWAR KOMATI's model, with a 74% baseline accuracy, as our benchmark since it uses the Universal Sentence Encoder for balanced accuracy and computational efficiency in processing social media text for suicidal ideation detection, serving as a practical reference for our study.

Comparative Studies. As shown in Fig. 9, we directly compared our machine models to those developed by RUTUJA POTDAR [14], who used XgBoost, KNN, Random Forest, and Naive Bayes. Our models outperformed hers across all evaluation metrics. This success is attributed to our comprehensive feature extraction strategies, including readability scores, sentiment analysis, and LDA topic features, in addition to basic text tokens and text length. We also employed RandomSearchCV for in-depth feature selection and hyperparameter optimization. Moreover, our Bi-LSTM's bidirectional architecture and use of the Adam optimizer resulted in noticeable improvement over Singh's model [15]. Lastly, our BERT model sets a new performance benchmark, exceedingly even the 95% standard set by Aldhyani et al. in their CNN-BiLSTM model [13]. The enhanced performance of our BERT model over Bi-LSTM highlights BERT's capability in understanding contextual relationships in text data. Unlike Bi-LSTM, BERT's attention mechanism better grasps semantic associations between words, vital for detecting subtle suicidal ideation indicators. Our tailored fine-tuning further honed BERT's classification accuracy. Through careful hyperparameter optimization and model adaptation, we maximized BERT's potential, setting a new benchmark in the field.

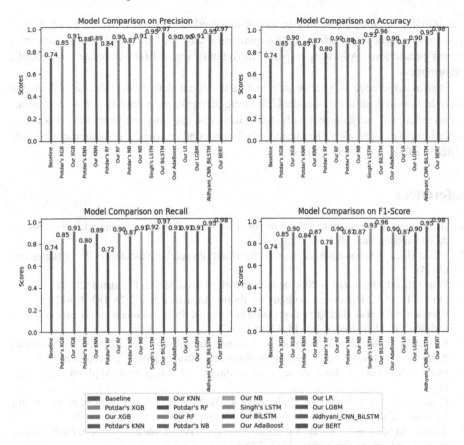

Fig. 9. Comparative Excellence: Our Models Outperform in Suicidal Ideation Detections

6   Conclusion

In conclusion, our study is critically important for the timely intervention in cases of suicidal ideation and sets a new standard in the field. We have made substantial advancements in both topic analysis and keyword extraction, adding an additional layer of depth to our research. Moreover, our machine learning models not only exceeded established benchmarks but also outperformed similar models in the field. However, it was our deep learning techniques that truly broke new ground. Our Bi-LSTM model achieved a validation accuracy of 97%, effectively capturing complex textual sequences. Most notably, our BERT model set an unprecedented benchmark by reaching a remarkable accuracy of 98%.

7   Future Work

Our study highlights the need for advancing suicide interventions, vital for public health. Our initial findings pave the way for further exploration. We aim to utilize advanced NLP models like GPT-4 for improved accuracy and deeper linguistic understanding, with transfer learning promising to unveil nuanced semantics. Enhancing our dataset by including data from various digital platforms can provide richer context, improving our predictions. Adjusting to platform dynamics could further refine our model's performance.

Ethical adherence is vital in mental health signal detection within social media, given the sensitive nature of suicide. Upholding data privacy is crucial. Our interventions should reflect empathy, respect individual narratives, and integrate supportive resources. As we improve our models, the ultimate goal transcends statistical enhancement, aiming at timely life-saving interventions.

References

1. Giachanou, A., Crestani, F.: Like it or not: a survey of Twitter sentiment analysis methods. ACM Comput. Surv. **49**, 1–41 (2016)
2. World Health Organization, Geneva, Switzerland: Preventing Suicide: A Global Imperative (2014)
3. World Health Organization: Suicide in the World: Global Health Estimates (2019)
4. O'Dea, B., et al.: Detecting suicidality on Twitter. Internet Interv. **2**(2), 183–188 (2015)
5. Guntuku, S.C., et al.: Detecting depression and mental illness on social media: an integrative review. Curr. Opin. Behav. Sci. **18**, 43–49 (2017)
6. Rajesh, D., Priya, V.K.: Consequences of Facebook on student's mental health - A Conceptual Analysis. Vels Institute of Science Technology and Advanced Studies, December 2019
7. Desmet, B., Hoste, V.: Emotion detection in suicide notes. Exp. Syst. Appl. **40**, 6351–6358 (2013)
8. Oussous, A., Benjelloun, F.-Z., Lahcen, A.A., Belfkih, S.: ASA: a framework for Arabic sentiment analysis. J. Inf. Sci. **46**, 544–559 (2019)
9. Tadesse, M.M., Lin, H., Xu, B., Yang, L.: Detection of suicide ideation in social media forums using deep learning. Algorithms **13**, 7 (2020)
10. Braithwaite, S.R., Giraud-Carrier, C., West, J., Barnes, M.D., Hanson, C.L.: Validating machine learning algorithms for Twitter data against established measures of suicidality. JMIR Mental Health **3**(2), e21 2015
11. Tadesse, M.M., Lin, H., Xu, B., Yang, L.: Detection of depression-related posts in Reddit social media forum. IEEE Access **7**, 44883–44893 (2019)
12. Singh, C., Imam, T., Wibowo, S., Grandhi, S.: A deep learning approach for sentiment analysis of COVID-19 reviews. Appl. Sci. **12**, 3709 (2022)
13. Aldhyani, T.H.H., Alsubari, S.N., Alshebami, A.S., Alkahtani, H., Ahmcd, Z.A.T.: Detecting and analyzing suicidal ideation on social media using deep learning and machine learning models. Int. J. Environ. Res. Pub. Health **19**(19), 12635 (2022)
14. Potdar, R.: Suicide Text Classification NLP. Kaggle (n.d.). https://www.kaggle.com/rutujapotdar/suicide-text-classification-nlp
15. Singh, A.: Suicidal Thought Detection. Kaggle (n.d.). https://www.kaggle.com/code/abhijitsingh001/suicidal-thought-detection
16. Komati, N.: Universal Sentence Encoder 74% accuracy sparknlp. Kaggle, 3 years ago. https://www.kaggle.com/code/nikhileswarkomati/universal-sentence-encoder-74-accuracy-sparknlp
17. Barton, C.: Analyzing suicidal text using natural language processing. All Graduate Plan B and other Reports, no. 1640 (2022)

P-Reader: A Clue-Inspired Model for Machine Reading Comprehension

Jiahao Kang, Liang Yang(✉), Yuefan Sun, Yuan Lin, Shaowu Zhang,
and Hongfei Lin

Dalian University of Technology, Dalian, China
{kangjiahao,syf}@mail.dlut.edu.cn,
{liang,zhlin,zhangsw,hflin}@dlut.edu.cn

Abstract. With the widespread use of web applications, a large amount of textual content is generated on the Internet continuously. In order to analyze and mine the information contained in the text, machine reading comprehension (MRC) is receiving increasingly more attention. As an important technique, MRC can boost the business value of Internet applications. Traditional MRC models use an extractive approach, resulting in poor performance on unanswerable questions. To address this problem, we propose a clue-inspired MRC model. Specifically, we mimic the human reading comprehension process through a combination of sketchy and intensive reading. Experimental results show that the proposed model achieves better performance on several public datasets, especially for unanswerable questions.

Keywords: Machine reading comprehension · Clue-inspired model · External knowledge base

1 Introduction

Reading comprehension is typically described as "the process of extracting and constructing the semantics of an article from written text through interaction." The purpose of the research is to use artificial intelligence to give computers the same reading comprehension ability as people. The Machine reading comprehension (MRC) task is specifically a method of extracting pertinent responses from unstructured documents in accordance with inquiries. As a result, scientists typically formalize MRC as a supervised learning question about the "document, question, answer" triplet. It can be classified into four task kinds based on the distinct answer forms: extraction, generation, cloze, and multiple choice.

MRC research has practical value in areas like information extraction and intelligent customer service due to its ability to efficiently process large amounts of text data, allowing users to quickly identify relevant information while reducing manual information acquisition costs. Traditional retrieval-based question

This work is supported by the grant from the National Social Science Foundation of China (No. 21BXW047).

answering systems often lead to redundant information, but MRC techniques enable a true understanding of the user's query based on the content of the article, including understanding historical comments and generating answers to current queries.

Currently, there are three types of extractive reading comprehension models: models based on attention mechanisms [1,2], pre-trained language models, and inference mechanisms.

Early methods for machine reading comprehension are based on attention mechanism. Seo et al. [3] discovered and improved the existing attention mechanism in the field of MRC, and proposed the Bidirectional Attention Flow (BIDAF) network. Upon its proposal, the BIDAF model attained unparalleled results on the SQuAD 1.1 dataset [4]. Wang et al. [5] proposed R-Net, which self-matches the question-aware paragraph representation to extract evidence from the entire passage using both passage words and question information.

With the rapid development of pre-trained models, MRC model based on pre-trained language models has achieved marvellous results on many datasets. Pre-trained language models can be divided into two categories: autoregressive language models [6,7] and autoencoding language models [8].

Moreover, inspired by human reading comprehension processes, a growing amount of work has introduced reasoning mechanisms into machine reading comprehension models. Sukhbaatar et al. [9] first proposed the MRC model that introduced the reasoning mechanism. Shen et al. [10] proposed the ReasoNet model that mimics the human reasoning process by focusing attention on different parts of the passage each time.

Despite the great success of some existing approaches based on pre-trained language models, they perform poorly on unanswerable questions due to the lack of human-like reasoning mechanisms. Furthermore, since pre-trained language models learn a general domain knowledge during pre-training, they perform poorly on short text machine reading comprehension datasets that require domain-specific knowledge. We propose a clue-inspired reading comprehension framework to address the above problems.

In summary, the contributions of this paper are as follows:

- We propose a reading comprehension framework that combines a sketchy reading module and an intensive reading module to simulate the human clue inpspired reading comprehension process.
- To address the poor performance of existing methods in solving domain-specific reading comprehension of short texts, we integrate a knowledge base into the model to empower the model with domain knowledge.
- Extensive experiments demonstrate that our method achieves comparable performance with some state-of-the-art methods, and even surpassing them in some metrics, which demonstrates the superiority of our method.

2   P-Reader

Zhang et al. [11] proposed for the first time a fine-tuning reading comprehension model called Retro-Reader, which includes two stages: sketchy reading and intensive reading, simulating human reading comprehension thinking.

2.1   Model Design

This paper focuses on extractive reading comprehension tasks, which can be described in the form of triplets (P, Q, A), where P represents the passage (context in the dataset), Q represents the query, and A represents the answer. A should be the original text directly extracted from the corresponding P. Our model should predict the start and end positions in the passage and extract A based on the given query. For queries that do not have an answer in the original passage, we need to output unanswerable conclusions.

We select RoBERTa [12] as our backbone model, and improve the Retro-Reader to further simulate the human clue-inspired reading comprehension process. An extractive MRC model P-Reader is proposed, including four parts: sketchy reading, intensive reading, knowledge enhancement, and joint training.

In the sketchy reading stage, the model browses the article and questions, creating a keyword set. During intensive reading, it extracts answers using keywords and external knowledge. Validation combines reading and final scores to provide the conclusive answer. See Fig. 1 for the model structure.

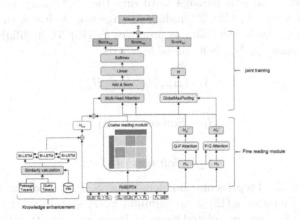

Fig. 1. P-Reader model structure.

Sketchy Reading Module. In the sketchy reading module, Q and P are used as inputs, where P represents the user comment and Q represents the queries raised by the annotator regarding the user comment. [CLS] and [SEP] tokens are added between Q and P to distinguish the content of Q and P. After being encoded by the RoBERTa model, it enters the sketchy reading module. The embedding used to represent text sequences is obtained through the RoBERTa model and context-aware linguistic feature are obtained. The sketchy reading module will extract keyword information from queries and passage. The embedding structure is shown in Fig. 2.

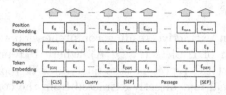

Fig. 2. Embedding structure.

In sketchy reading, this paper proposes a keyword-aware algorithm, which aims to help the model to determine the keywords in the query and the relevant key parts in the passage, as well as the keywords in the passage and the relevant important parts in the query, so that the model can perceive the key content in the text.

This paper utilizes RoBERTa model to create embeddings, H_Q for query and H_P for passage. We compute word similarity between query and passage using a trilinear function, creating matrix $S \in \mathbb{R}^{m \times n}$ (Equation 1). S_{ij} represents similarity between the i-th passage word and the j-th query word. Applying softmax to rows yields S_1 (Eq. 2), finding passage words closest to query words. Similarly, softmax applied to columns produces S_2 (Eq. 3), highlighting relevant query words in passage. W_S is a trainable matrix.

$$S = W_S(H_P, H_Q, H_P \cdot H_Q) \tag{1}$$

$$S_1 = \text{Softmax} \rightarrow (S) \tag{2}$$

$$S_2 = \text{Softmax} \downarrow (S) \tag{3}$$

The contextualized representation, denoted as S_{QKey}, is computed by averaging S_1 towards the passage (Eq. 4) to highlight query statement keywords. Then, pivotal segments in passage, related to query keywords, are attended to yield A_P (Eq. 5). Crucial segments are emphasized and integrated into the context vector via element-wise multiplication denoted by $\otimes$ (Eq. 6).

$$S_{QKey} = \text{mean} \downarrow (S_1) \tag{4}$$

$$A_P = S_2 \cdot S_{QKey} \tag{5}$$

$$H_{PKey} = H_P + H_P \otimes A_P \tag{6}$$

Equation 7 averages S_2 towards query words, emphasizing passage keywords. Attention mechanism identifies crucial query word segments related to these keywords, yielding A_Q (Eq. 8). It also highlights pivotal query word segments, integrating them into query word representation, creating a problem-specific representation enriched with key information. Finally, the query embedding integrated with passage keyword information, H_{QKey}(Equation 9), is obtained.

We add H_{PKey} and H_{QKey} as sketchy reading module output, $H_{Sketchy}$, for further usage.

$$S_{PKey} = \text{mean} \rightarrow (S_2) \tag{7}$$

$$A_Q = S_1 \cdot S_{PKey} \tag{8}$$

$$H_{QKey} = H_Q + H_Q \otimes A_Q \tag{9}$$

Intensive Reading Module. Consider human reading comprehension process. After determining the scope of the answer to a query through sketchy reading, humans tend to leverage intensive reading to further eliminate irrelevant information and pinpoint the answer to the question accurately. To further simulate this process, we introduces Q2P and P2Q modes based on diverse reading habits. The model integrates these modes, facilitating knowledge acquisition from varied perspectives. This approach tackles context-free reading comprehension, enhancing nuanced subject understanding.

In Q2P mode, for each word Q_i in Q, we use the attention from the pre-generated paragraph sequence H_P to calculate it. Then, merge the representations H_P in the paragraph through attention. Finally, we will add $\tilde{H}_{Q_i}$ back to H_Q ultimately to obtain representation H'_Q, as shown in Eqs. 10 to 12.

$$\alpha_{i,j} = \frac{\exp(H_{P_j} H_{Q_i}^T)}{\sum_j^{l_p} \exp(H_{P_j} H_{Q_i}^T)} \tag{10}$$

$$\tilde{H}_{Q_i} = \sum_j^{l_p} \alpha_{i,j} H_P \tag{11}$$

$$H'_{Q_i} = H_{Q_i} + \tilde{H}_{Q_i} \tag{12}$$

In P2Q mode, for each word P_i in P, we use the attention from the pre-generated paragraph sequence H_Q to calculate it. Then, merge the representations H_Q in the paragraph through attention. Finally, we will add $\tilde{H}_{P_i}$ back to H_P ultimately to obtain representation H'_P, as shown in Eqs. 13 to 15.

$$\alpha_{i,j} = \frac{\exp(H_{Q_j} H_{P_i}^T)}{\sum_{j=1}^{l_p} \exp(H_{Q_j} H_{P_i}^T)} \tag{13}$$

$$\tilde{H}_{P_i} = \sum_{j}^{l_q} \alpha_{i,j} H_Q \tag{14}$$

$$H'_{P_i} = H_{P_i} + \tilde{H}_{P_i} \tag{15}$$

Finally, with intensive reading module, we obtained the output of Q-P Attention H'_Q and P-Q Attention H'_P. The design of Q-P Attention and P-Q attention not only covers common sense models of reading comprehension, but also reduces the influence of irrelevant verbs on individual words, and through the information exchange of attention, these patterns no longer lack overall semantic knowledge.

Knowledge Enhancement. This paper focuses on MRC for short text, where user comments in datasets like Res and RRC are typically under 200 words. With short inputs, the model struggles with word semantics and unclear pronoun references. Human readers rely on memory to supplement comprehension, enhancing correct answers. To improve MRC's understanding, leveraging external knowledge is crucial. This paper integrates open-source knowledge bases for enhanced comprehension.

This paper extracts user comments from the Chinese Dianping Review Dataset (4.4 million comments from 540,000 users in 240,000 restaurants) [13–16] and the English Yelp dataset[1] in the catering domain. Data was processed, retaining reviews, removing irrelevant details, and desensitizing user info, resulting in knowledge bases for Chinese (9.7 MB) and English (4 GB) restaurant domains.

This paper uses a retrieval-based knowledge embedding method for external knowledge. Each word in the Q and P is matched with K related words in comments, forming input for joint training. Words in Q and P are treated as tokens. For each token S_i, related KB concepts $(C(S_i))$ are retrieved and encoded using bidirectional LSTM. The resulting vectors, H_P and H_Q, are concatenated as H_{Out}, providing contextual and external knowledge information.

Joint Training. The joint training of P-Reader involves fusing intensive reading vectors, conducting binary classification $(score_{ext})$ for answerability. Sketchy reading keywords and enhanced knowledge are integrated with intensive reading output for Multi-Head Attention. Regularization and Softmax are applied, generating $score_{has}$ and $score_{null}$. These scores, along with $score_{ext}$, determine answerability and provide the final answer.

The P-Reader model addresses the challenge of predicting both answer positions and detecting unanswerable questions. It determines question answerability

---

[1] https://www.yelp.com/dataset.

through P2Q and Q2P readings. Sketchy reading keywords and external knowledge are combined with P2Q and Q2P module outputs. If answerable, the model outputs the answer, combining the results for the final answer.

In the first phase of joint training, this paper concatenates vectors H'_Q and H'_P. The model judges the paragraph's ability to answer the question by evaluating the special token representation $H_{[CLS]}$. This vector serves as an overall interrogative sentence representation. It undergoes Linear layer processing, using cross entropy for binary classification. Equations 16 and 17 represent answerability for N samples. The difference, $score_{ext} = logit_{na} - logit_{ans}$, is a crucial indicator in subsequent validations.

$$\hat{y}_i = \text{Softmax}(\text{Linear}(H_{[CLS]})) \tag{16}$$

$$\mathcal{L}^{ans} = -\frac{1}{N} \sum_{i=1}^{N} [y_i \log \hat{y}_i + (1 - y_i) \log(1 - \hat{y}_i)] \tag{17}$$

In the second phase of joint training, H_{Out} is combined with sketchy reading keywords representation $H_{Sketchy}$ to create H_{join}. Using multi-head Attention with H_{join}, H'_Q, and H'_P as inputs, vector H' is obtained (Eq. 18).

$$H' = \text{SoftMax}(\text{Linear}(\text{Attention}(H'_Q, H'_P, H_{join}))) \tag{18}$$

In the third phase of joint training, start and end positions are predicted using vector H'. Combined with $score_{ext}$, this determines whether the answer of the query could be extracted from the passage. MRC aims to find the answer span; probabilities s and e are obtained from H' using Softmax (Eq. 19). Training involves cross entropy loss for start and end predictions (Eq. 20), where y_i^s and y_i^e represent positions of Example i. N is the number of examples.

$$s, e \propto \text{Softmax}(\text{FFN}(H')) \tag{19}$$

$$\mathcal{L}^{span} = -\frac{1}{N} \sum_{i=1}^{N} [\log p_{y_i^s}^s + \log p_{y_i^e}^e] \tag{20}$$

At the same time, this paper further judges whether the question can be answered according to the vector H', so that the reader can also identify the answerable question. This paper uses three loss function: cross entropy loss, binary cross entropy loss and regression mean square error loss to verify. The representation h'_1 in the vector H' is passed to the fully connected layer to obtain classification logic and regression scores.

(1) Cross entropy is used as the loss function of classification verification, where K represents the number of classes ($K = 2$ in the work of this paper, N represents the number of examples, as shown in Eqs. 21 and 22.

$$\overline{y}_{i,k} = \text{Softmax}(\text{FFN}(h'_1)) \tag{21}$$

$$\mathcal{L}^{ans} = -\frac{1}{N}\sum_{i=1}^{N}[y_i \log \overline{y}_i + (1-y_i)\log(1-\overline{y}_i)] \tag{22}$$

(2) Use the binary cross entropy loss function as the classification verification loss function. As shown in Eqs. 23 and 24.

$$\overline{y}_i = \sigma(\text{FFN}(h_1')) \tag{23}$$

$$\mathcal{L}^{ans} = -\frac{1}{N}\sum_{i=1}^{N}\sum_{k=1}^{K}[y_{i,k}\log \overline{y}_{i,k}] \tag{24}$$

(3) The mean square error is used as its loss function. As shown in Eqs. 25 and 26.

$$\overline{y}_i = \text{FFN}(h_1') \tag{25}$$

$$\mathcal{L}^{ans} = -\frac{1}{N}\sum_{i=1}^{N}[(y_i - \overline{y}_i)^2] \tag{26}$$

During the training period, this paper adopts a joint weighted training method of span loss and validation loss, as shown in Eq. 27.

$$\mathcal{L} = \alpha_1 \mathcal{L}^{span} + \alpha_2 \mathcal{L}^{ans} \tag{27}$$

Subsequently, this paper adopts a threshold based answerable verification, which is a heuristic strategy used to determine whether the question is answerable based on the predicted answer start and end logic. Given the probability of output starting and ending, as well as the possibility of verification v, we can calculate the scores based on both answerable scores $score_{has}$ and unanswerable scores $score_{null}$, as shown in Eqs. 28 and 29.

$$score_{has} = \max(s_k + e_l), 1 \le k \le l \le n \tag{28}$$

$$score_{null} = s_1 + e_1 \tag{29}$$

This paper adopts the difference between $score_{has}$ and $score_{null}$ as the final unanswered score, $score_{diff}$, $score_{diff} = score_{null} - score_{has}$. Set and determine answerable thresholds δ based on the development set. This model predicts that if the final score is above the threshold, the answer span of the answer score will be given, otherwise the conclusion that the question cannot be answered will be given. The threshold based answerability verification is adopted as the final step in answerability decisions in all of our models. The calculation of the threshold is shown in Eq. 34, where β_1 and β_2 are weight parameters that provides a predicted answer when v is greater than δ, otherwise the conclusion that the problem cannot be answered is output.

$$v = \beta_1 score_{diff} + \beta_2 score_{ext} \tag{30}$$

3 Experiments

This section first introduces the hyperparameter setting of the P-Reader model proposed in this paper, then introduces the selection and setting of the baseline model, and finally analyzes the comparative experimental results between the model in this paper and the baseline model, as well as various aspects of demonstration models such as ablation experiments, sub experiments and sample analysis.

3.1 Experimental Setup

This paper conducts experiments on the extracted subset of the self-made Res dataset. The Res (sp) dataset distinguishes between versions v1 and v2 based on whether the question can be answered. Considering the generalization of the model, this paper extends the P-Reader model to the SQuAD1.0 dataset [4] and SQuAD2.0 dataset [17] to verify the effectiveness of the model.

The Res dataset focuses on catering industry comments, collected through crawlers from a public review app. Data is filtered for compliance and length. One annotator raises a question, two provide answers in the text. To mitigate annotator bias, a fourth annotator filters pairs as the final dataset version.

The Res dataset consists of two sub datasets: the extractive sub dataset Res (sp) and the generative sub dataset Res (qa). The extractive sub dataset consists of two versions. In version v1, the answers to all questions can be directly extracted from the original text. In version v2, the dataset adds unanswerable questions, that is, questions that cannot be directly found in the original text need to be answered unanswerable.

In our implementation, the max sequence length is set to 256. During the training phase, the batch size, learning rate, dropout probability are set to 16, 2e−5, 0.1, respectively. The model is trained for 10 epochs.

3.2 Baseline Model

This paper selects the BERT model and RoBERTa model that performed well on the self-made Res dataset, the improved ALBERT and ELECTRA models based on the BERT model, and the Retro-Reader model that was first proposed for sketchy reading and intensive reading as the baseline model for this experiment to compare with the model in this paper, as follows:

(1) BERT-base [8]: Fine tune the pre-trained model BERT-base.
(2) RoBERTa-base [12]: Fine tune the pre-trained model RoBERTa-base.
(3) ALBERT [18]: By using parameter reduction technology to reduce memory consumption and accelerate BERT training speed, a self supervised loss is introduced to model sentence coherence.

Table 1. Experimental results on Res (sp) dataset.

Model	Res(sp)_v1		Res(sp)_v2	
	EM	F1	EM	F1
BERT-base	71.37	79.04	61.98	67.05
ALBERT	72.78	81.60	62.83	69.64
ELECTRA	72.09	80.87	64.09	70.23
RoBERTa-base	74.01	81.94	65.00	72.51
Retro-Reader on ALBERT	74.89	81.06	67.35	73.76
Retro-Reader on ELECTRA	75.64	82.31	68.98	74.07
P-Reader	**76.64**	**85.98**	**71.26**	**77.31**

(4) ELECTRA [19]: A new replaced token detection task has been proposed, which greatly improves the speed of the model while maintaining performance.

(5) Retro-Reader [11] on ALBERT: A Retro-Reader model that uses the ALBERT model as a sketchy and intensive reading encoder.

(6) Retro-Reader [11] on ELECTRA: A Retro-Reader model that uses the ELECTRA model as a sketchy and intensive reading encoder.

3.3 Experimental Analysis

The experimental results of the P-Reader model and baseline model proposed in this paper on the Res (sp) dataset are shown in Table 1.

Experimental results demonstrate that in traditional pre-trained models, ALBERT and ELECTRA outperform BERT on Res(sp)_v1 and Res(sp)_v2 datasets, achieving higher efficiency with fewer parameters and training time. However, RoBERTa exhibits superior accuracy and F1 score due to its deeper layers and larger parameter scale. Yet, its extended training time poses challenges. Addressing this balance between performance and parameters remains a pressing issue.

The models that adopt the idea of sketchy reading and intensive reading have higher EM and F1 performance than the models that do not. On Res(sp)_v2 dataset, the Retro-Reader model based on ALBERT improves EM and F1 by 2.35% and 1.25% compared with RoBERTa-base model; the Retro-Reader model based on ELECTRA improves EM and F1 by 3.98% and 1.56% compared with RoBERTa-base model, while the improvement on Res(sp)_v1 dataset is much smaller. This paper believes that compared with traditional models such as BERT and RoBERTa, the models that adopt the design idea of sketchy reading and intensive reading can significantly improve the model's reading comprehension ability. At the same time, since the Retro-Reader model focuses on unanswerable questions, the improvement on v2 dataset is more significant, which also indicates that the model with two-stage verification of sketchy reading and intensive reading can improve experimental results while maintaining a low number of parameters.

This paper is based on the RoBERTa base model and combines the P-Reader model constructed by human clue-inspired reading comprehension process, achieving the optimal experimental results in the experiment. Compared to the Retro Reader model based on ELECTRA, in two different versions of dataset experiments, the P-Reader-large model improved the EM index by 1.00% and 2.28%, and the F1 index by 3.67% and 3.24%, respectively. This indicates that the P-Reader model proposed in this paper can further fit the human reading process and improve the ability to solve MRC problems in specific fields compared to the Retro-Reader model.

In order to further validate the effectiveness and generalization of the P-Reader model, this paper conducted experiments on the publicly available datasets SQuAD1.1 and SQuAD2.0 in the field of MRC. The experimental results are shown in Table 2.

Table 2. Experimental results on SQuAD dataset

Model	SQuAD1.1		SQuAD2.0	
	EM	F1	EM	F1
BERT-base	83.20	90.40	77.60	80.40
RoBERTa-base	88.90	94.60	86.50	89.40
ALBERT	82.30	89.30	77.10	80.00
ELECTRA	84.50	90.80	80.50	83.30
Retro-Reader on ALBERT	–	–	88.10	91.40
Retro-Reader on ELECTRA	–	–	**89.60**	**92.10**
P-Reader	**89.13**	**95.30**	89.42	91.85

The experimental results show that the P-Reader model proposed in this paper achieves the optimal results in the SQuAD1.1 dataset. This indicates that using efficient pre-trained models and introducing domain related knowledge in MRC tasks in specific fields can improve the experimental results to a certain extent, proving the effectiveness of the P-Reader model structure.

On the SQuAD2.0 dataset, the P-Reader model proposed in this paper has improved EM and F1 metrics by 2.92% and 2.45% compared to the RoBERTa-base model. The P-Reader model has significant advantages in solving unanswerable queries through sketchy reading, intensive reading, and joint training of the model structure, further verifying the effectiveness of the model structure. Compared with the Retro-Reader model based on the ELECTRA model, there are 0.18% and 0.25% gaps in EM and F1 indicators, which indicates that the P-Reader model proposed in this paper has similar performance with the Retro-Reader model in reading comprehension in the general field. At the same time, sufficient general domain knowledge is used in the pre training, so introducing the general domain external knowledge base in fine-tuning model does not play a significant role.

Comparing the experimental results, it was found that the P-Reader model achieved lower returns on the SQuAD dataset compared to the Res dataset. This indicates that the P-Reader model is more suitable for short text MRC tasks in specific fields, and the benefits on traditional MRC datasets are not significant enough, proving the effectiveness of the P-Reader model in specific fields.

The P-Reader model proposed in this paper mainly includes three parts: Knowledge Enhancement (Enhance), sketchy reading (Sketchy), and intensive reading (Intensive). Three modules were removed from the P-Reader model for ablation experiments, as shown in Table 3.

Table 3. The ablation experiment of P-Reader on Res (sp) dataset

	Res(sp)_v1		Res(sp)_v2	
Model	EM	F1	EM	F1
P-Reader-base	76.08	84.98	70.92	75.76
w/o Enhance	73.13	82.74	67.26	74.15
w/o Sketchy	75.75	83.97	68.17	73.96
w/o Intensive	74.09	82.01	65.98	73.04

Experimental results show removing the knowledge augmentation module significantly impacts Res(sp)_v1 results, underlining its importance. Relevant comment information from external knowledge bases substantially boosts short text comprehension. Further analysis will explore the impact of selected user comments and delve deeper into the module's role.

In the Res(sp)_v2 dataset, removing the intensive reading module has the most significant impact, hindering joint training for unanswerable questions. This leads to decreased accuracy on Res(sp)_v2. This emphasizes the effectiveness of the joint training mechanism proposed in this paper for unanswerable queries. Removing the sketchy reading module resulted in accuracy drops of 1.01% and 1.8% on Res(sp)_v1 and Res(sp)_v2, respectively. Despite its smaller impact compared to the intensive reading module, it enhances keyword extraction akin to human thinking during initial reading. This affirms the necessity and effectiveness of each P-Reader module.

This paper aims to further investigate the impact of the number of external comments retrieved in the knowledge enhancement module on the P-Reader model. Therefore, a comparative study and analysis of the number of retrieved comments K are conducted, as shown in Fig. 3.

The experimental results show that as the number of search comments K increases, the experimental accuracy shows a trend of first increasing and then decreasing. When the number of comments K = 5, the experimental accuracy is the highest. This indicates that integrating product comments from external

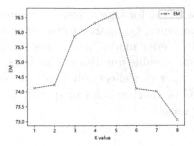

Fig. 3. Influence of K value on experimental results.

knowledge bases in the P-Reader model has a promoting effect on the model. However, as the number of integrated user comments increases, the P-Reader model learns more external information, which may interfere with the model due to deviations from the comment information in the dataset or the integration of information with lower relevance to the problem, resulting in a decrease in experimental accuracy. Therefore, selecting an appropriate number of external comments in the knowledge augmentation module has a significant impact on the performance of the model. If too many comments are integrated, it will actually lead to a decrease in experimental results.

It can be seen that the BERT model and RoBERTa model gain low accuracy on the v2 dataset. The main reason for the low accuracy on the v2 dataset is the low accuracy of answering unanswerable questions that require logical reasoning. The Retro-Reader model proposes a two-stage reading approach to improve the accuracy of unanswerable questions. Therefore, this paper analyzes and compares the accuracy of the P-Reader model and the Retro-Reader model on different question types, as shown in Fig. 4.

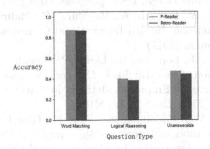

Fig. 4. Comparison of accuracy rates for different question types.

The P-Reader model on the Res(sp)_v2 dataset has an accuracy of 87.04% for word matching question types, 39.91% for logical reasoning question types, and 47.31% for unanswerable question types. It can be seen that compared to the Retro-Reader model, the P-Reader model has improved by 0.47% for word matching question types, 1.70% for logical reasoning question types, and 2.75% for unanswerable question types. Compared to the improvement in word matching problem types, the P-Reader model has a more significant improvement in logical reasoning and unanswerable questions. This indicates that the P-Reader model proposed in this paper can effectively solve problems that require deep logical reasoning in MRC of short articles in specific fields and problems that cannot be answered in datasets.

4 Conclusion

In this paper, we focus on the task of extractive MRC. On the basis of the Retro-Reader model, we further simulate the clue-inspired thinking process and construct a P-Reader model that includes knowledge enhancement, sketchy reading, intensive reading, and joint training modules. Experimental results show that the P-Reader model is more suitable for MRC tasks in specific fields. In future work, we plan to explore more forms of reading comprehension tasks, such as generative reading comprehension tasks, cloze reading comprehension tasks, and multiple choice reading comprehension tasks. Additionally, we will investigate the generalization of our model structure to other datasets and explore the possibility of simulating more human reading comprehension processes to improve our model.

References

1. Bahdanau, D., Cho, K., Bengio, Y.: Neural machine translation by jointly learning to align and translate. In: 3rd International Conference on Learning Representations, ICLR, San Diego (2015)
2. Vaswani, A., et al.: Attention is all you need. In: Advances in Neural Information Processing Systems, Long Beach, USA, pp. 5998–6008 (2017)
3. Seo, M.J., Kembhavi, A., Farhadi, A., Hajishirzi, H.: Bidirectional attention flow for machine comprehension. In: 5th International Conference on Learning Representations, ICLR, Toulon (2017)
4. Rajpurkar, P., Zhang, J., Lopyrev, K., Liang, P.: Squad: 100, 000+ questions for machine comprehension of text. In: Su, J., Carreras, X., Duh, K. (eds.) Proceedings of the 2016 Conference on Empirical Methods in Natural Language Processing, EMNLP, Austin, pp. 2383–2392. ACL (2016)
5. Wang, W., Yang, N., Wei, F., Chang, B., Zhou, M.: Gated self-matching networks for reading comprehension and question answering. In: Proceedings of the 55th Annual Meeting of the Association for Computational Linguistics, ACL, Vancouver, Volume 1: Long Papers, pp. 189–198. ACL (2017)
6. Peters, M.E., et al.: Deep contextualized word representations. In: Proceedings of the 2018 Conference of the North American Chapter of the Association for Computational Linguistics: Human Language Technologies, NAACL-HLT, New Orleans, Volume 1 (Long Papers), pp. 2227–2237. ACL (2018)
7. Radford, A., Wu, J., Child, R., Luan, D., Amodei, D., Sutskever, I., et al.: Language models are unsupervised multitask learners. OpenAI Blog 1(8), 9 (2019)

8. Devlin, J., Chang, M., Lee, K., Toutanova, K.: BERT: pre-training of deep bidirectional transformers for language understanding. In: Proceedings of the 2019 Conference of the North American Chapter of the Association for Computational Linguistics: Human Language Technologies, NAACL-HLT, Minneapolis, Volume 1 (Long and Short Papers), pp. 4171–4186. ACL (2019)
9. Sukhbaatar, S., Szlam, A., Weston, J., Fergus, R.: End-to-end memory networks. In: Advances in Neural Information Processing Systems, Montreal, pp. 2440–2448 (2015)
10. Shen, Y., Huang, P., Gao, J., Chen, W.: ReasoNet: learning to stop reading in machine comprehension. In: Proceedings of the 23rd ACM SIGKDD International Conference on Knowledge Discovery and Data Mining, Halifax, pp. 1047–1055. ACM (2017)
11. Zhang, Z., Yang, J., Zhao, H.: Retrospective reader for machine reading comprehension. In: The 35th AAAI Conference on Artificial Intelligence, AAAI, 33rd Conference on Innovative Applications of Artificial Intelligence, IAAI, The 11th Symposium on Educational Advances in Artificial Intelligence, EAAI, Virtual Event, pp. 14506–14514. AAAI Press (2021)
12. Liu, Y., et al.: RoBERTa: a robustly optimized BERT pretraining approach. CoRR abs/1907.11692 (2019). http://arxiv.org/abs/1907.11692
13. Zhang, Y., Zhang, M., Liu, Y., Ma, S., Feng, S.: Localized matrix factorization for recommendation based on matrix block diagonal forms. In: 22nd International World Wide Web Conference, WWW 2013, Rio de Janeiro, pp. 1511–1520. International World Wide Web Conferences Steering Committee/ACM (2013)
14. Zhang, Y., Zhang, M., Liu, Y., Ma, S.: Improve collaborative filtering through bordered block diagonal form matrices. In: Jones, G.J.F., Sheridan, P., Kelly, D., de Rijke, M., Sakai, T. (eds.) The 36th International ACM SIGIR Conference on Research and Development in Information Retrieval, SIGIR 2013, Dublin, pp. 313–322. ACM (2013)
15. Zhang, Y., Zhang, H., Zhang, M., Liu, Y., Ma, S.: Do users rate or review?: Boost phrase-level sentiment labeling with review-level sentiment classification. In: The 37th International ACM SIGIR Conference on Research and Development in Information Retrieval, SIGIR 2014, Gold Coast, pp. 1027–1030. ACM (2014)
16. Zhang, Y., Lai, G., Zhang, M., Zhang, Y., Liu, Y., Ma, S.: Explicit factor models for explainable recommendation based on phrase-level sentiment analysis. In: The 37th International ACM SIGIR Conference on Research and Development in Information Retrieval, SIGIR 2014, Gold Coast, pp. 83–92. ACM (2014)
17. Rajpurkar, P., Jia, R., Liang, P.: Know what you don't know: unanswerable questions for squad. In: Proceedings of the 56th Annual Meeting of the Association for Computational Linguistics, ACL, Melbourne, Volume 2: Short Papers, pp. 784–789. ACL (2018)
18. Lan, Z., Chen, M., Goodman, S., Gimpel, K., Sharma, P., Soricut, R.: ALBERT: a lite BERT for self-supervised learning of language representations. In: 8th International Conference on Learning Representations, ICLR, Addis Ababa (2020)
19. Clark, K., Luong, M., Le, Q.V., Manning, C.D.: ELECTRA: pre-training text encoders as discriminators rather than generators. In: 8th International Conference on Learning Representations, ICLR 2020, Addis Ababa, Ethiopia (2020)

An Unsupervised Method for Sarcasm Detection with Prompts

Qihui Lin[1], Chenwei Lou[1], Bin Liang[2], Qianlong Wang[1], Zhiyuan Wen[1],
Ruibin Mao[3], and Ruifeng Xu[1(✉)]

[1] School of Computer Science and Technology, Harbin Institute of Technology
(Shenzhen), Shenzhen, China
`21b351012@stu.hit.edu.cn`, `xuruifeng@hit.edu.cn`
[2] The Chinese University of Hong Kong, Hong Kong, China
`bin.liang@cuhk.edu.hk`
[3] Shenzhen Securities Information Co., Ltd., Shenzhen, China
`maoruibin@cninfo.com.cn`

Abstract. Sarcasm detection is challenging in natural language processing since its peculiar linguistic expression. Thanks in part to the availability of considerable annotated resources for some datasets, current supervised learning-based approaches can achieve promising performance in sarcasm detection. In real-world scenarios, annotating data for the peculiar language expression of sarcasm proves challenging. Consequently, recent studies have delved into unsupervised learning approaches for sarcasm detection, seeking to mitigate the labor-intensive process of annotation. In this paper, we present a novel unsupervised sarcasm detection method leveraging abundant unlabeled social media data. Our approach revolves around employing prompts as a cornerstone. Initially, we gathered approximately 3 million texts from Twitter through targeted hashtag-based searches, segregating them into sarcasm and non-sarcasm categories based on associated hashtags. Subsequently, these collected texts undergo training using a pre-trained BERT model, customized for masked language modeling and coined as **SarcasmBERT**. This step aims to enhance the model's grasp of sarcastic cues within the text. Finally, we devise prompts tailored for the unlabeled data to execute unsupervised sarcasm detection effectively. Our experimental findings across six benchmark datasets highlight the superiority of our method over state-of-the-art unsupervised baselines. Additionally, the integration of our SarcasmBERT into established BERT-based sarcasm detection methods showcases a direct avenue for enhancing performance, thereby illustrating its potential for immediate and substantial improvements.

Keywords: unsupervised sarcasm detection · pre-trained language model · prompt · sentiment analysis

1 Introduction

Sarcasm, as a complex language phenomenon, often masks true sentiments behind literal meanings. This intriguing yet prevalent expression significantly

X. Pan et al. (Eds.): ICCC 2023, LNCS 14207, pp. 34–46, 2024.
https://doi.org/10.1007/978-3-031-51671-9_3

impacts sentiment analysis and stance detection in social networks. Consequently, sarcasm detection has garnered extensive attention within the realm of natural language processing. The core challenge lies in identifying the disparities between the literal text expression and its underlying emotional intent, which characterizes sarcasm detection efforts.

In recent years, the landscape of sarcasm detection has witnessed a surge in methodological advancements [1–3,9,11,14,15,17,18,21]. Within the realm of supervised approaches, prior methodologies have endeavored to discern sarcastic clues by modeling inconsistent contextual information [3,8,18] or leveraging lexical features [15]. Moreover, attempts have been made to exploit external knowledge in understanding the patterns of sarcasm within sentences [5,14]. Despite considerable strides in this domain, supervised methods heavily rely on copious annotated datasets. Yet, annotating sufficient data across various domains, especially those with limited resources, remains labor-intensive due to the adaptable and context-specific nature of sarcastic expressions. Therefore, recent efforts have delved into the realm of unsupervised learning to tackle sarcasm detection. Some studies focus on text reconstruction and subsequent comparison with the original text's emotional context, aiming to unveil incongruities inherent in the atypical expression of sarcasm [10,21]. However, these endeavors often overlook a fundamental gap existing between common corpora such as BooksCorpus [16], commonly used in models like BERT, and the peculiarities of sarcasm-laden data, a distinctive and nuanced verbal expression. This discrepancy poses a significant challenge in effectively training models to discern and interpret sarcasm accurately.

To tackle these challenges, we introduce SarcasmBERT, an unsupervised sarcasm detection method designed to bridge the gap between pre-trained language models and the intricate task of sarcasm detection. Our approach involves leveraging a vast repository of unlabeled Twitter data to enhance BERT's learning of sarcastic nuances, thereby obviating the need for manual annotation. Initially, we curate a comprehensive corpus from Twitter using targeted hashtag keyword searches, marking texts as sarcasm or non-sarcasm based on specific words like "sarcasm," "sarcastic," "irony," or "ironic," while utilizing stop-words for non-sarcasm texts. This yields around 3 million English Tweets, each tagged with either a sarcasm or non-sarcasm hashtag. To refine the data and address potential hashtag errors, we employ data augmentation techniques to enhance data quality. Then we employ the masked language modeling (MLM) task to further pre-train BERT using this Twitter corpus, resulting in the creation of SarcasmBERT-a language model specifically attuned to detecting sarcastic nuances. Finally, leveraging the knowledge acquired by SarcasmBERT, we construct prompts tailored to predict hashtag categories and directly discern whether a given text embodies sarcasm or not. This approach effectively enables the model to extrapolate its learning to identify sarcasm without relying on explicit annotations.

The main contributions of our work are summarized as follows:

– To the best of our knowledge, we are the first to introduce sarcastic information into BERT for sarcasm detection, coined as SarcasmBERT.

- The proposed SarcasmBERT can be directly used to detect sarcastic expressions without any annotation.
- A series of experiments on publicly available sarcasm detection benchmark datasets including Twitter [17,18], IAC [15], and Reddit [11], show that our proposed SarcasmBERT achieves the state-of-the-art performance on unsupervised sarcasm detection.
- Further, experimental results in the supervised scenario show that our SarcasmBERT can be combined with existing supervised sarcasm detection models and achieve improved performance.

2   Method

This section provides an in-depth exploration of our method, spanning from the collection of data to sarcasm-aware BERT pre-training, culminating in sarcasm detection. The model framework is visually depicted in Fig. 1. Our model consists of three core components: Twitter Data Acquisition, Sarcasm-aware Pre-training, and Sarcasm Detection. We initiate the process by curating an extensive Twitter dataset, followed by augmenting a pre-trained language model, BERT, through specialized sarcasm-aware pre-training methodologies. Subsequently, this refined model is deployed to discern sarcasm within textual data. During the detection phase, inputs are meticulously formatted to align with our training data structure. Leveraging the language model's capabilities, our model outputs classification labels that categorize the text into sarcastic or non-sarcastic labels.

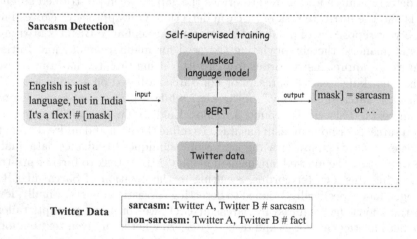

Fig. 1. Illustration of our proposed method.

2.1 Twitter Data

We crawl Twitter texts from Twitter Search API by keyword searches with the TweetScraper tool[1]. We divide Twitter data into two categories (sarcasm and non-sarcasm). And use the hashtag (#) on Twitter as an indicator of texts. The #sarcasm, #sarcastic, #irony, and #ironic hashtags are used to identify sarcasm tweets. Then tweets without these hashtags are considered to be non-sarcastic. In addition, we keep only the sarcasm-related hashtag and move the hashtag to the end of the text.

However, labels are only a hint, they are not exact labels, which introduces a lot of noise and leads to poor model results. Therefore, we use data augmentation methods to minimize the impact of such errors. Two Twitter texts with the same hashtag category are connected and the common hashtag is used as the label for the connected texts. Assuming that the probability of noise due to inaccurate labeling is α, then the probability of noise in the merged text is:

$$\alpha' = \alpha * \alpha \quad (0 < \alpha < 1) \tag{1}$$

where α' is significantly smaller than α. Therefore, this method can reduce the noise probability and improve the model performance. We also swap the order of the spliced text to eliminate the effect of the upper afternoon caused by the splicing order. In addition, in order to unify the format of sarcastic and non-sarcastic texts, the tag #fact is added at the end of non-sarcastic texts. the whole data processing process is shown in the following Fig. 2. Twitter A and Twitter B are two spliced texts. We finally obtained 1.8 million tweets with sarcasm tags and 1.6 million tweets with factual tags, which provides rich expressions and data support for the sarcasm detection task.

2.2 Sarcasm-Aware Pre-training

In the process, we sarcasm-aware pre-training the language model BERT based on large-scale Twitter data. BERT's model architecture [7] is a multi-layer bidirectional Transformer encoder based on [20], which uses the multi-head self-attention mechanism to capture context information. We initialize the model with BERT pre-trained weights and choose the BERT task, masked language modeling, to complete the training. The selection of the Masked Language Model (MLM) method for our continued pre-training serves as a deliberate strategic choice. This decision aligns seamlessly with the pre-training methodology employed by BERT, fortifying the language model's capacity to discern sarcasm without compromising its original capabilities. This synergy ensures a smoother transition into the realm of sarcasm detection. Furthermore, the self-supervised nature of the MLM training method harmonizes with the fundamental tenets of our proposed unsupervised sarcasm detection approach. By eliminating the need for manual labeling, it underscores our commit'ment to an unsupervised paradigm. Notably, the MLM model's inherent ability to discern relationships

---

[1] https://github.com/jonbakerfish/TweetScraper.

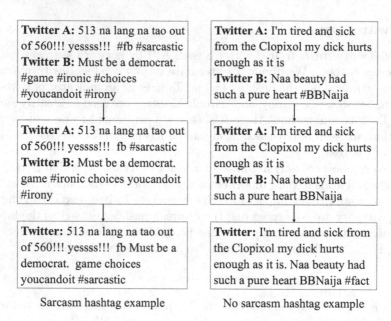

Fig. 2. Twitter data pre-process.

and contextual dependencies between words emerges as a pivotal asset. It equips the model to not only comprehend the individual meanings of words but also appreciate their nuanced roles within a given context. This, in turn, empowers the model to detect a broader spectrum of satirical patterns and enhance prediction accuracy, surpassing the outcomes of manually constructed contextual relationships.

2.3   Sarcasm Detection

To leverage the results of pre-training the language model BERT and sarcasm-aware pre-training on top of it, we design the prediction form of the downstream task to narrow the gap between pre-training and the sarcasm detection task. Instead of considering sarcasm detection as a classification task, we transfer it to a masked word prediction task closer to the masked language model task in the sarcasm-aware pre-training phase. Following the data processing phase, a pattern of hashtags follows each text, and for each test sample, a # prompt is added at the end of the text to guide the model to predict the subsequent hashtag. Then the prediction results are mapped to two groups of pre-labels #sarcasm, #irony, #sarcastic, #ironic, and #fact, which denote sarcasm and non-sarcasm, respectively. In this way, the model can distinguish whether the text is sarcastic or not.

What's more, solving an unsupervised task becomes much easier when we give a task or training data description. So we add a prompt #Twitter at the end of each text to explain the characteristics of data that the model trained on. In this way, the model obtains more information from the training phase and can overcome the drawback of a single data source, which applies to satire detection data from different platforms. In summary, the prompt construction for sarcasm detection is shown in Fig. 3.

Twitter: Finals week is going to be awesome now that I can' t even grip a pencil #fml $\longrightarrow$ **Prompt:** Finals week is going to be awesome now that I can' t even grip a pencil #fml #[mask]

Twitter: Yes, amazing, how they weren't people before. $\longrightarrow$ **Prompt:** Yes, amazing, how they weren't people before. # Twitter # [mask]

Fig. 3. Examples of prompt construction for sarcasm detection.

3 Experiments

To validate the effectiveness of the approach, we conduct extensive experiments.

3.1 Experimental Setup

Datasets. We conduct experiments on six sarcasm datasets from three different sources:

- Tiwtter: There are two datasets published by Riloff [18] and ptacek [17]. For the Twitter datasets, we retrieve tweets using the Twitter API with the provided tweet IDs[2].
- IAC (Internet Argument Corpus): There are two versions of the dataset collected by [15], which are denoted as IAC-v1[3] and IAC-v2[4] respectively.
- Reddit: We use two subsets (movies and technology) of the Reddit dataset provided by [11].

The statistics of the sarcasm datasets are shown in Table 1.

Settings. Our model is trained based on uncased $BERT_{base}$. Throughout the sarcasm-aware pre-training phase, we harness the computational power of 4 V100 GPUs (32 GB each) with a learning rate set at 5e-5. The batch size is configured to 16, the maximum sequence length is capped at 512, and a gradient accumulation step of 32 is employed. To optimize the model, we implement the Adam optimizer [12].

---

[2] http://api.twitter.com/.
[3] https://nlds.soe.ucsc.edu/sarcasm1.
[4] https://nlds.soe.ucsc.edu/sarcasm2.

Table 1. Statistics of training and test datasets.

Datasets	Train		Test	
	Sarcasm	Non	Sarcasm	Non
Twitter-1(Ptacek)	23,456	24,387	2,569	2,634
Twitter-2(Riloff)	282	1051	35	113
IAC-V1	862	859	97	94
IAC-V2	2,947	2,921	313	339
Reddit-1(movies)	5,521	5,607	1,389	1,393
Reddit-2(tech)	6,419	6,393	1,596	1,607

During the subsequent sarcasm detection phase, we deliberately exclude any data from the test or validation sets. Instead, we formulate prompts for each test data instance and input them directly into the model for prediction. The parameter configurations for this detection phase mirror those utilized in the pre-training procedure, ensuring consistency and reproducibility.

3.2 Comparison Baselines

1) **Lexicon:** Sarcasm is construed as an expression encompassing both positive and negative sentiments. To identify such expressions, we leverage SenticNet [6], which aids in pinpointing positive and negative words within the text. A sentence is deemed sarcastic if it contains a juxtaposition of positive and negative words.

2) **TF-IDF-LDA:** Sentence representation is obtained through TF-IDF [19], followed by data stratification into two clusters, namely sarcasm and non-sarcasm, utilizing the Latent Dirichlet Allocation (LDA) algorithm [4].

3) **TF-IDF-Kmeans:** Similar to TF-IDF-LDA, this method employs TF-IDF for sentence representation. However, the LDA algorithm is replaced with the K-Means [13] clustering algorithm to differentiate between sarcasm and non-sarcasm clusters.

4) **BERT:** Our approach involves employing a pre-trained language model, specifically BERT [7], for direct sarcasm prediction within an unsupervised framework.

5) **sent-MG:** As proposed by Wang et al. [21], this method utilizes a pre-trained generation model to reconstruct sentence components. Subsequently, similarity scores between the original and regenerated sentences, based on BERT representations, are computed to ascertain the presence of sarcasm.

6) **sent-MG + SimCSE:** An extension of 5), this method involves further fine-tuning of sentence representation through unsupervised contrast learning using the simCSE algorithm. This serves as an alternative enhancement to the initial BERT-based approach.

3.3 Main Experiment Results

Table 2 shows the experiment results on six benchmark datasets. Our method achieves sota results on all datasets except Twitter-2. For two Twitter datasets,

Table 2. Main experimental results on different datasets. The baseline results for comparison are obtained from [21], where the dataset partitioning and experimental environment closely align with our study. The best scores are in bold. The second-best scores are underlined.

MODEL	Twitter-1		Twitter-2		IAC-1		IAC-2		Reddit-1		Reddit-2	
	Acc.(%)	F1.(%)	Acc.(%)	F1.(%)	Acc.(%)	F1.(%)	Acc.(%)	F1.(%)	Acc.(%)	F1.(%)	Acc.(%)	F1.(%)
Lexicon [21]	59.00	55.86	57.43	52.7	47.64	40.29	44.01	39.12	43.06	42.71	42.77	41.47
TF-IDF-LDA [21]	54.52	54.36	50.68	48.15	53.40	53.22	54.61	52.44	52.51	50.81	51.72	47.65
TF-IDF-Kmeans [21]	52.27	44.1	**72.97**	51.86	49.73	49.35	51.68	47.52	49.68	46.74	52.58	43.29
BERT [7]	<u>59.46</u>	56.54	41.22	41.21	51.39	36.35	48.00	35.72	47.19	39.47	46.91	37.63
sent-MG [21]	50.21	52.35	67.57	55.24	52.35	53.75	62.06	56.75	52.62	52.60	51.92	49.89
sent-MG+SimCSE [21]	58.91	<u>58.76</u>	56.76	<u>58.31</u>	<u>57.59</u>	<u>55.44</u>	<u>64.30</u>	<u>64.27</u>	<u>53.30</u>	<u>54.91</u>	<u>56.16</u>	<u>56.14</u>
SarcasmBERT	**77.17**	**77.00**	<u>68.92</u>	**66.47**	**63.35**	**61.58**	**68.87**	**67.72**	**66.89**	**66.54**	**67.31**	**67.26**

which are from the same domain as our pre-training data, our method significantly outperforms previous unsupervised methods in all metrics except for the Acc. (%) metric on the Twitter-2 dataset, which is slightly lower than the performance of the TF-IDF-Kmeans method. This may be due to the fact that the Twitter-2 dataset is too small in size and there is some overfitting in our training approach. In particular, the Acc. and F1. values of SarcasmBERT on the Twitter-1 dataset are higher than the previous SOTA by 18.17% and 18.24%, respectively. For other datasets from different domains, our method far exceeds sent-MG + SimCSE and gets new state-of-the-art performances by adjusting the prompt. This implies that by enriching the dataset and pursuing extended pre-training, we can achieve robust sarcasm recognition within the language model. The best improvements are on the Reddit datasets, where the values of both Acc. and F1. metrics are more than 10% points higher than the previous best method.

3.4   Ablation Study

To analyze the impact of each step in the data processing, we conduct an ablation study in Table 3. In this section, we show the three important roles in data processing, which are concatenating two Twitter texts, swapping the order of the two concatenated texts, and adding hashtag #fact at the end of Twitter texts without #sarcasm, respectively. 1) w/o concat only uses one Twitter text with hashtags as a training sample instead of concatenating two Tweets and keeps the number of training data consistent by duplicated samples. 2) w/o swap does not exchange the position of two concatenated Twitter texts and maintains the training data scale by increasing the combination of concatenated texts. We can see that swapping can eliminate the effect of token position on model effectiveness. 3) w/o #fact does not add #fact after texts without sarcastic hashtags. The experiment implies that the uniform training data format has a significant effect on the model and unsupervised prediction.

Table 3. Ablation study (Acc.). concat denotes concatenating two Tweets. exchange denotes swapping the order of two concatenated Tweets. #fact denotes adding the fact hashtag at the end of a Twitter text.

MODEL	Twitter-1	Twitter-2	IAC-1	IAC-2	Reddit-1	Reddit-2
SarcasmBERT	**77.17**	68.92	63.35	68.87	**66.89**	**67.31**
w/o concat	75.25	**72.97**	**70.15**	**69.17**	65.22	65.74
w/o exchange	71.84	66.89	59.69	69.63	66.10	66.69
w/o #fact	49.38	23.65	50.79	48.01	49.83	49.93

4   Discussion

Impact of Self-supervised Learning on Performance. During collecting the Twitter dataset, we use hashtags in the tweets as remote tags to help distinguish between sarcastic and non-sarcastic texts. In the previous experiment, we use hashtags as part of the text and self-supervised training on the whole text. Here, we change to consider the hashtag as the label of a text where the text containing the sarcastic hashtag is taken as a positive sample and the text without such hashtag as a negative sample, then take supervised training on these Twitter data (based on BERT and the text classification task). We compare the two training methods and the result is shown in Table 4. We can find that the self-supervised method can improve performance. That means the self-supervised training approach allows the model to learn more about sarcastic expressions. What's more, the hashtag does not accurately mark whether the text expresses sarcasm or not, and the self-supervised training approach is better at eliminating this noise.

Table 4. The performance (Acc.) of different training methods on the Twitter dataset based on BERT. The first and second rows in the table indicate unsupervised training and supervised training, respectively.

MODEL	Twitter-1	Twitter-2	IAC-1	IAC-2	Reddit-1	Reddit-2
SarcasmBERT	77.17	68.92	63.35	68.87	66.89	67.31
supervised	74.21	45.95	60.73	64.88	65.56	66.81

Impact of Twitter Dataset Scale. To investigate the impact of the scale of the Twitter dataset, we set different data scales, randomly retaining 20%, 40%, 60%, and 80% of the Twitter data as the data set for further pre-training and observing the model's performance in downstream tasks. As shown in Fig. 4, sarcasm detection (accuracy) got better as the data size increased on most of the downstream datasets. When the data size was 100%, more outstanding results could be achieved. In particular, on the Twitter-2 (Ptacek) dataset, the experimental results tended to decrease with increasing data size, with the highest accuracy being achieved with only 20% of the data retained. This may be due to the specificity of this dataset, which is small and in the same Twitter domain. A large amount of pre-trained data can lead to over-fitting of the model and thus loss of generalization ability. Furthermore, it's important to note that this method's scope is constrained by the exclusive use of Twitter as the primary data source, neglecting other domains and textual varieties. Expanding the dataset to encompass diverse sources and text types is an avenue for future research, enabling the model to acquire a more comprehensive understanding of nuanced ironic expressions.

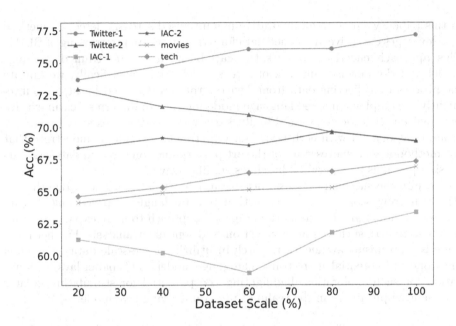

Fig. 4. Impact of Twitter data scale.

Table 5. The performance (Acc.) of ADGCN-BERT and replacing BERT with SarcasmBERT.

MODEL	Twitter-1	Twitter-2	IAC-1	IAC-2	Reddit-1	Reddit-2
ADGCN-BERT	88.20	83.78	69.11	79.91	78.22	78.11
-SarcasmBERT	88.91	86.48	71.73	79.14	78.79	79.05

Impact of SarcasmBERT for Supervised Method. To assess the effectiveness of SarcasmBERT, we conduct experiments by substituting the pre-trained language model in a supervised method with SarcasmBERT. A comparative analysis is then performed between the performance of ADGCN-BERT, a state-of-the-art model for supervised sarcasm detection, and ADGCN-SarcasmBERT. The outcomes, detailed in Table 5, indicate that ADGCN-SarcasmBERT consistently outperforms ADGCN-BERT across multiple datasets. These findings underscore SarcasmBERT's role as a specialized pre-trained language model tailored for sarcasm detection tasks, presenting itself as a valuable plug-in to enhance the overall performance of the model.

5 Conclusion

In this paper, we present an innovative unsupervised sarcasm detection method that leverages extensive unlabelled data for sarcasm-aware pre-training of BERT. This approach effectively bridges the gap between the pre-trained language model and the downstream task of sarcasm detection. Specifically, we initiate the process by collecting data from Twitter through targeted hashtags. Subsequently, we employ a masked language modeling task to discern sarcasm expressions within the collected data. Finally, sarcasm detection is executed based on prompts associated with each text. Our experimental results demonstrate that our methodology achieves state-of-the-art performance on sarcasm datasets, surpassing previous unsupervised baselines significantly.

Despite the success in sarcasm detection, it's crucial to acknowledge the relatively narrow scope of this task within natural language processing. Future endeavors should aim to extend the proposed approach to more expansive application scenarios, such as stance detection and sentiment analysis. Furthermore, there is a promising avenue for research in utilizing large-scale data to broaden the scope and potential of pre-trained language models. This paper lays the foundation for such exploration, highlighting the potential for stimulating greater scope and applicability in the realm of pre-trained language models.

Acknowledgment. This work was partially supported by the Key Technologies Research and Development Program of Shenzhen JSGG20210802154400001, Shenzhen Foundational Research Funding JCYJ20220818102415032, and the Joint Lab of HITSZ and China Merchants Securities.

References

1. Agrawal, A., An, A.: Affective representations for sarcasm detection. In: The 41st International ACM SIGIR Conference on Research & Development in Information Retrieval, pp. 1029–1032 (2018)
2. Agrawal, A., An, A., Papagelis, M.: Leveraging transitions of emotions for sarcasm detection. In: Proceedings of the 43rd International ACM SIGIR Conference on Research and Development in Information Retrieval, pp. 1505–1508 (2020)
3. Bamman, D., Smith, N.: Contextualized sarcasm detection on twitter. In: Proceedings of the International AAAI Conference on Web and Social Media vol. 9, pp. 574–577 (2015)

4. Blei, D.M., Ng, A.Y., Jordan, M.I.: Latent dirichlet allocation. J. Mach. Learn. Res. **3**, 993–1022 (2003)
5. Cambria, E., Li, Y., Xing, F.Z., Poria, S., Kwok, K.: Senticnet 6: ensemble application of symbolic and subsymbolic AI for sentiment analysis. In: Proceedings of the 29th ACM International Conference on Information and Knowledge Management, pp. 105–114 (2020)
6. Cambria, E., Speer, R., Havasi, C., Hussain, A.: Senticnet: a publicly available semantic resource for opinion mining. In: 2010 AAAI Fall Symposium Series (2010)
7. Devlin, J., Chang, M.W., Lee, K., Toutanova, K.: Bert: pre-training of deep bidirectional transformers for language understanding. In: Proceedings of the 2019 Conference of the North American Chapter of the Association for Computational Linguistics: Human Language Technologies, Volume 1 (Long and Short Papers), pp. 4171–4186 (2019)
8. González-Ibánez, R., Muresan, S., Wacholder, N.: Identifying sarcasm in twitter: a closer look. In: Proceedings of the 49th Annual Meeting of the Association for Computational Linguistics: Human Language Technologies, pp. 581–586 (2011)
9. Jena, A.K., Sinha, A., Agarwal, R.: C-net: contextual network for sarcasm detection. In: Proceedings of the Second Workshop on Figurative Language Processing, pp. 61–66 (2020)
10. Joshi, A., Agrawal, S., Bhattacharyya, P., Carman, M.J.: *Expect the Unexpected*: harnessing sentence completion for sarcasm detection. In: Hasida, K., Pa, W.P. (eds.) PACLING 2017. CCIS, vol. 781, pp. 275–287. Springer, Singapore (2018). https://doi.org/10.1007/978-981-10-8438-6_22
11. Khodak, M., Saunshi, N., Vodrahalli, K.: A large self-annotated corpus for sarcasm. arXiv preprint arXiv:1704.05579 (2017)
12. Kinga, D., Adam, J.B.: Adam: a method for stochastic optimization (2015)
13. Lloyd, S.: Least squares quantization in PCM. IEEE Trans. Inf. Theory **28**(2), 129–137 (1982)
14. Lou, C., Liang, B., Gui, L., He, Y., Dang, Y., Xu, R.:. Affective dependency graph for sarcasm detection. In: Proceedings of the 44th International ACM SIGIR Conference on Research and Development in Information Retrieval, pp. 1844–1849 (2021)
15. Lukin, S., Walker, M.: Really? well. apparently bootstrapping improves the performance of sarcasm and nastiness classifiers for online dialogue. arXiv preprint arXiv:1708.08572 (2017)
16. Panayotov, V., Chen, G., Povey, D., Khudanpur, S.: Librispeech: an asr corpus based on public domain audio books. In: 2015 IEEE international conference on acoustics, speech and signal processing (ICASSP), pp. 5206–5210. IEEE (2015)
17. áš Ptáček, T., Habernal, I., Hong, J.: Sarcasm detection on Czech and English twitter. In: Proceedings of COLING 2014, the 25th International Conference on Computational Linguistics: Technical papers, pp. 213–223 (2014)
18. Riloff, E., Qadir, A., Surve, P., De Silva, L., Gilbert, N., Huang, R.: Sarcasm as contrast between a positive sentiment and negative situation. In: Proceedings of the 2013 Conference on Empirical Methods in Natural Language Processing, pp. 704–714 (2013)
19. Karen Sparck Jones: A statistical interpretation of term specificity and its application in retrieval. J. Document. **28**(1), 11–21 (1972)

20. Vaswani, A.: Attention is all you need. In: Advances in Neural Information Processing Systems, 30 (2017)
21. Wang, R., et al.: Masking and generation: an unsupervised method for sarcasm detection. In: Proceedings of the 45th International ACM SIGIR Conference on Research and Development in Information Retrieval, pp. 2172–2177 (2022)

ENER: Named Entity Recognition Model for Ethnic Ancient Books Based on Entity Boundary Detection

Lifeng Zhao, Ziquan Feng[✉], Na Sun, and Yong Lu

School of Information Engineering, Minzu University of China, Beijing, China
22301990@muc.edu.cn

Abstract. Due to the significant differences between the entity identification rules in the field of ethnic ancient books and the existing methods, the general model has poor accuracy in identifying specific terms in the field entity extraction task and fails to effectively solve the problems of ambiguity and nesting of Chinese entities by using boundary information. In this paper, we construct a small-scale named entity corpus of ethnic ancient books and propose an Ethnic Naming Entity Recognition (ENER) model integrating entity boundary detection. In ENER, BERT model is used to pre-train the corpus of ancient book text annotation, Bidirectional Gate Recurrent Unit (BiGRU) encodes the contextual features of ancient books. Conditional Random Field (CRF) adds an auxiliary task of entity boundary detection based on named entity identification task to enhance model's ability to identify entity boundaries and generates the named entity tag sequence of ancient books. Experiments on the corpus of ancient books named entities and other general Chinese data sets show the effectiveness of our approach. On the one hand, ENER has improved the accuracy, recall and F1 value by 2.09%, 1.62% and 1.85% respectively. Compared with the baseline BERT-BiLSTM-CRF model and achieved higher indicators than other models. On the other hand, ENER shows better effect on the recognition of ancient book named entities in small-scale corpus and it is also stable on Chinese general data sets. It can be applied in dealing with text containing specific terms in the ethnic field and promoted to more tasks in the future.

Keywords: Named entity recognition · Digitization of ancient books · ENER · Entity boundary detection · Corpus

1 Introduction

Named Entity Recognition (NER) [1] was first proposed as a clear concept at the Sixth Message Understanding Conferences (MUC-6) in November 1995. The NER task aims to extract proprietary terms from a given sentence. Since MUC-6, the task of identifying basic nouns has been more carefully divided. For example, people's names can be further subdivided into categories such as writers and actors, and place names can be further subdivided into categories such as countries, provinces, and towns. At present,

X. Pan et al. (Eds.): ICCC 2023, LNCS 14207, pp. 47–59, 2024.
https://doi.org/10.1007/978-3-031-51671-9_4

named entity recognition plays an important role as the key support for the downstream applications of natural language processing technologies such as relationship extraction [2] and information retrieval. Due to less ambiguity in the annotation of general domain data, entities are usually flat structure and simple composition rules. Therefore, there are many achievements in representative fields such as agriculture [3], medicine [4], military [5], geology [6], and the named entity recognition technology has made good research progress.

For ethnic ancient books, the extraction of terms such as the names of ethnic minorities, place names, work names, and collection units is the basis for the construction of the knowledge base of ancient books. On the one hand, the carrier forms of ancient books of ethnic minorities are diverse. The use of digital technology based on entity extraction can better protect the information of endangered ancient books [7]; On the other hand, the extracted ancient book entities can help researchers analyze the complex relationships between historical figures.

It is worth noting that entity recognition of ethnic ancient books belongs to the "low resource" field of Chinese named entity recognition, lacking relevant annotation training sets and corpora. In addition, the names of ethnic minorities and common names are quite different. General models are difficult to identify the names such as "阿育史坡 (Ayushi Po)", "沙马尔铁 (Shamar Tie)" and "吉日呷呷 (Jiri Gaga)". It poses a greater challenge to the existing Chinese NER model. To this end, we establish a small corpus of annotation for ethnic minority ancient books and propose an Ethnic Naming Entity Recognition (ENER) model based on named entity recognition task and entity boundary detection subtask. To verify the effectiveness of the model, we conduct experiments on the established corpus and the general Chinese NER dataset and achieve excellent results.

Overall, the main contributions of this article are as follows: (1) Establishing an ethnic ancient book NER corpus and providing resources for the follow-up work in this field. (2) Combining boundary detection task with NER task and effectively improves the accuracy of naming entity recognition in ethnic ancient books.

Section 2 first gives the related work. Section 3 gives the overall structure of the model, the algorithm principle of each part and the loss function of model training. Section 4 details and analyzes the experimental results. Section 5 summarizes the problems of ENER model in the entity recognition of ethnic ancient books and looks forward to its future development direction.

2 Related Work

Named entity recognition technology can be divided into rule-based methods, statistical model-based methods, and deep learning-based methods according to its development [8]. In the early named entity recognition task, the method based on rule and statistical machine learning is simple and feasible [9–11]. For example, Li Na et al. established an automatic alias extraction model based on conditional random fields by analyzing the internal and external characteristics of aliases in local records corpus [11]. The recognition rate of alias, place name and reference name are significant, and the overall accuracy rate is 93.52%.

Since Hinton and his team first proposed the concept of deep learning in 2006 [12] and pointed out that the solution of deep neural network training problem can be solved through layer-by-layer initialization, deep learning has begun to emerge in the task of named entity recognition with its powerful feature learning ability. In recent years, with the continuous development of deep learning research, the methods of entity extraction and recognition began to focus on various deep learning models, and the methods based on pre-training model achieved the most advanced performance [13–18]. Liu et al. proposed the automatic extraction method of traditional music term entities based on BERT, LSTM, CRF and other models [13]. Based on the manual annotation and construction of the corpus of traditional music terms, they compared and analyzed the performance of CRF, LSTM, LSTM-CRF and BERT in the task of entity extraction such as inheritor and instrument naming in music text. The average F1 value of the model reached 91.77%, which achieved good results. Zhou et al. Introduced Albert pretraining model and multi head self-attention mechanism into BiLSTM-CRF model [17], which improved the accuracy of scene, imagination and other entitics cxtraction in ancient poetry and reduced the training time by 19.56%.

Although there have been a lot of excellent research results in the field of ancient book named entity recognition, most of them ignore the use of entity boundary in-formation. Li et al. pointed out that the entity boundary detection task is highly related to the named entity recognition task, which can help the model effectively learn the entity boundary information [19]. They used a model training method of sharing parameter information and achieved good results on the English social media dataset twitter-2015, in which the F1 value reached 73.57%. Chen [20] et al. Proposed a method to add the graph attention network layer to capture the dependencies between words in sentences and add the prediction of the first and last words of entities to the training as an auxiliary task. Experiments on general data sets show that the entity recognition accuracy and boundary judgment have been significantly improved.

In this paper, establishing a corpus of annotation of ancient books of ethnic minorities. We focus on the special needs of ancient book entity extraction, propose a recognition method combined with entity boundary detection to improve the effect of minority ancient book entity recognition.

3   ENER: Model for Identifying Named Entities in Ethnic Minority Ancient Books

In this paper, we propose an Ethnic Named Entity Recognition (ENER) model that integrates entity boundary information to solve the problem of poor recognition effect of nested entities and named entities in the field of minority ancient books. Its structure is shown in Fig. 1.

It is mainly composed of four parts: text preprocessing layer, feature learning layer, context coding layer and multitask learning layer. The input text sentence is split, and length controlled by the text preprocessing layer to get the corresponding character sequence. Based on the BERT pre-training model, the feature learning layer optimizes the parameters for the task of national ancient book text named entity recognition and obtains the vector sequence with ancient book text semantic features. The context encoding layer

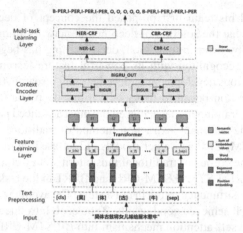

Fig. 1. Structure diagram of ENER model.

uses BiGRU network to capture context information. After linear transformation and label relation feature learning of text feature vector through two branches in the multitask learning layer, named entity recognition and entity boundary label sequences can be obtained. The training module divides the entity recognition task into two objectives: entity recognition loss optimization and entity boundary recognition loss optimization.

3.1 Text Preprocessing Algorithm

The function of the text preprocessing layer is to convert the ancient text to be recognized into a finite length character sequence to meet the input requirements of the Bert model in the feature learning layer. The definition of text preprocessing algorithm is shown as follow:

$$f^{Pre} = Input \rightarrow X\left(Input, X \in R^{n \times 1}\right) \tag{1}$$

where input is the text of ancient books to be recognized, X is the character sequence obtained after preprocessing the input text, and N is the text length. Details are shown in Algorithm 1:

Algorithm 1: How to preprocess the text

Input: Text of ancient books to be recognized
Output: Finite-length character sequence X={X1, X2, ..., Xn}
1 initialization: Max-len: Maximum length of output sequence;
2 Segmentation of the input text;
3 **if** *length of the text >Max-len - 2* **then**
4 | Truncate the sequence at position Max-len - 2;
5 **else**
6 | No Action;
7 **end**
8 add two special marks [CLS] and [SEP] at the beginning and end of the character sequence;

3.2 Feature Learning Algorithm

BERT [21] is a pre-trained language model based on bidirectional Transformers. After learning the semantic information of text, it can solve the problems of entity nesting and semantic complexity to a certain extent (Fig. 2).

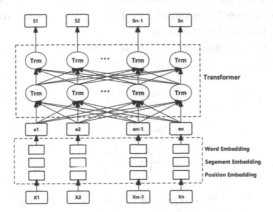

Fig. 2. Structure of Feature learning layer.

The feature learning layer first constructs the corresponding unique heat vector according to the position information of ancient text characters in the dictionary and the original sentence. We suppose that the three unique heat vectors corresponding to the i-th character are $e_i^t \in R^{1 \times v}$, $e_i^s \in R^{1 \times s}$, $e_i^p \in R^{1 \times n}$. The process of converting them into word vectors e_i^{word}, block vectors e_i^{seg}, position vectors e_i^{pos} and adding together to obtain the input vector e_i can be expressed as following:

$$e_i^{word} = e_i^t W_t \tag{2}$$

$$e_i^{seg} = e_i^s W_s \tag{3}$$

$$e_i^{pos} = e_i^p W_p \tag{4}$$

$$e_i = e_i^{word} + e_i^{seg} + e_i^{pos} \tag{5}$$

where W_t, W_s, W_p represent the trainable word vector matrix, block vector matrix and position vector matrix respectively, V and S denote the size of the vocabulary and block code of the word.

Input the vector list $E = \{e_1, e_2, \ldots, e_n\}$ into the BERT coding layer, and the semantic association between the members in the character list X is fully learned through the multi-layer transform structure. Finally we obtain the semantic vector information list $S = \{s_1, s_2, \ldots, s_n\}$. Where $s_i \in R^{1 \times b}$, b is the hidden layer dimension(768 by default).This process can be formally expressed as:

$$f^{BERT} = X \rightarrow S\left(X \in R^{n \times 1}, S \in R^{n \times b}\right) \tag{6}$$

3.3 Context Encoding Algorithm

GRU network combines the forgetting gate and input gate of LSTM network into update gate. It not only achieves similar performance effect with the latter, but also reduces the time cost of training, and has better generalization ability on small sample data sets. The research work shows that the bidirectional loop network is better than the feedforward loop network in the sequence annotation task. In this paper, we use BiGRU network to capture the statement context information.

The hidden state of semantic vector s_i in BiGRU and the process to get vector list $H = \{h_1, h_2, \ldots, h_n\}$ can be expressed as (Fig. 3):

$$\overrightarrow{h_i} = \overrightarrow{GRU}(s_i) \tag{7}$$

$$\overleftarrow{h_i} = \overleftarrow{GRU}(s_i) \tag{8}$$

$$h_i = \left[\overrightarrow{h_i}, \overleftarrow{h_i}\right] \tag{9}$$

$$f^{GRU} = S \rightarrow H\left(S \in R^{n \times b}, H \in R^{n \times 2 \times hidden}\right) \tag{10}$$

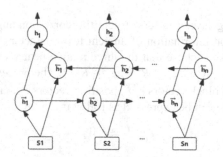

Fig. 3. Context encoder network structure

Where $\overrightarrow{h_i}$ and $\overleftarrow{h_i}$ represent the preceding and following information captured by GRU network, [] denotes concatenating two vectors.

3.4 Multitask Learning Algorithm

In the multitask learning layer, we linearly change the vector list output from the BiGRU network and transfer it to the named entity recognition CRF layer and entity boundary detection CRF layer in the multitask learning layer to learn the dependencies between tags.

Suppose that the ancient book entity to be identified corresponds to a total of M labels. In the named entity recognition branch of the multitask learning layer, the vector list is first linearly transformed (It is recorded as NER-LC) to obtain the vector list L:

$$f^{NER-LC} = H \rightarrow L\left(H \in R^{n \times 1}, L \in R^{n \times m}\right) \tag{11}$$

For $L = \{L_1, L_2, \ldots, L_n\}$, the predicted NER label sequence can be represented as $y = \{y_1, y_2, \ldots, y_n\}$. The predicted score and probability are:

$$Score(L, y) = \sum_{i=0}^{n} A_{y_i, y_{i+1}} + \sum_{i=1}^{n} P_{i, y_i} \tag{12}$$

$$P(y, L) = \frac{\exp(Score(L, y))}{\sum_{y^{\sim} \in Y_L} \exp(Score(L, y^{\sim}))} \tag{13}$$

P_{i, y_i} is probability that the i-th character is marked as y_i. $A_{y_i, y_{i+1}}$ is the transition probability from y_i to y_{i+1}. Y_L is the set containing all possible NER label sequences (Fig. 4).

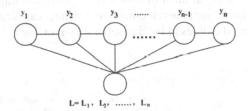

Fig. 4. CRF structure in named entity recognition branch.

Similarly, in the branch of entity boundary detection, the vector list H is converted to L'. The process is recorded as CBR-LC:

$$f^{CBR-LC} = H \rightarrow L'\left(H \in R^{n \times 1}, L' \in R^{n \times c}\right) \tag{14}$$

where C represents the number of types of entity boundary labels. For example, if BIO annotation mode is adopted, the value of C is 3. For boundary sequences y', the predicted score and probability are:

$$Score(L', y') = \sum_{i=0}^{n} A_{y_{i'}, y_{i+1'}} + \sum_{i=1}^{n} P_{i, y_{i'}} \tag{15}$$

$$P(y', L') = \frac{\exp(Score(L', y'))}{\sum_{y'^{\sim} \in Y_{L'}} \exp\left(Score\left(L', y'^{\sim}\right)\right)} \tag{16}$$

3.5 Model Learning

In training, the goal is to maximize the probability P (y, L) to obtain a more accurate sequence of NER labels. We design the loss function based on log likelihood. Considering that the loss of entity boundary detection is too large or too small, which can affect the learning of the main task, we set its weight in the total loss to 0.5. The loss function of model training is:

$$Loss = -\frac{1}{N} \sum_{i=0}^{N} P(y, L) - 0.5 * \frac{1}{N} \sum_{i=0}^{N} P(y', L') \tag{17}$$

4 Experiment and Result Analysis

4.1 Corpus Construction

In this paper, we take the "Outline of the General Catalogue of Chinese Ethnic Minority Ancient Books" as the knowledge source. We select 2217 representative ancient book entries for preprocessing and obtain a total of about 500000 words of ethnic minority ancient book texts based on manual text grammar check and format conversion. Next, we use the Label Studio tool to annotate five types of named entity in ancient texts: place name (LOC), collection organization (ORG), person name (PER), publishing organization (PRESS), and work name (WORK). We have labeled a total of 26254 ethnic ancient book named entities and stored them in BIO format. After labeling, the proportion of each type of entity in the training, development, and testing sets is approximately 8:1:1. The distribution of named entities in the dataset is shown in Table 1 (Fig. 5).

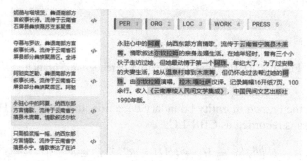

Fig. 5. The annotation examples.

Table 1. Statistical distribution of entities in the ancient book dataset.

	LOC	ORG	PER	PRESS	WORK	TOATAL
Train set	5155	1708	6133	1011	2599	16606
Validation set	1305	644	1624	378	775	4726
Test set	1351	700	1681	384	806	4922

4.2 Evaluation Indexes and Experimental Environment

In this paper, we use accuracy (P), recall (R) and F1 score to evaluate the effectiveness of the model.

$$P = \frac{T_P}{T_F} * 100\% \tag{18}$$

$$R = \frac{T_P}{T_N} * 100\% \tag{19}$$

$$F_1 = \frac{2PR}{P+R} * 100\% \tag{20}$$

where T_P represents the number of entities correctly identified by the model, T_F represents the number of entities identified by the model, T_N represents the number of entities in the test set, and F_1 is the harmonic average of accuracy and recall rate.

The experiment in this paper uses Pytorch lightning 1.5.10 framework and python3.6.7 environment for training and testing. The processor is the 11th generation Intel Core i5-11400h @ 2.70 GHz, and the memory size is 16 GB. The specific training parameter settings are shown in Table 2.

Table 2. Parameters settings.

Parameters	Value
Embedding dim	768
Hidden dim	128
Learning rate	5e−05
Drop-out	0.5
batch-size	20
weight decay	9e−3

4.3 Results and Analysis

To verify the effectiveness of ENER, we compare the classic named entity recognition baseline model and adds ablation experiment analysis to the network of each layer of the model.

Table 3. Results of different models in Ancient Books Inheritance Dataset.

Model	Precision	Recall	F1 value
BiLSTM-CRF	84.52%	85.55%	85.03%
BiGRU-CRF	82.47%	85.05%	83.74%
BERT-CRF	86.01%	86.87%	86.43%
BERT-BiLSTM-CRF	89.76%	88.48%	89.12%
BERT-BiGRU-CRF	89.31%	89.74%	89.53%
ENER	**91.85%**	**90.10%**	**90.97%**

The results are shown in Table 3. Compared with the baseline model BiLSTM-CRF, ENER and other models have improved their generalization ability, accuracy and recall rate due to the use of the BERT pre-training representation learning layer. Compared with LSTM model, GRU model has the advantages of simple structure and less parameters. Although the accuracy of BERT-BiGRU-CRF model is 0.45% lower than BERT-BiLSTM-CRF, the recall rate of the former is 1.26% higher than that of the latter and has better F1 index. Significantly, after adding the auxiliary task of entity boundary detection, the accuracy, recall and F1 value of ENER model were improved by 2.54%, 0.36% and 1.44% respectively compared with BERT-BiGRU-CRF model. The results show that ENER can further improve the effect of entity recognition after making full use of entity boundary information.

At the same time, we analyze the experimental results of each entity type in ENER. It has achieved good recognition results in person name, works, publishers and press. The best effect of entity recognition is the works entity, Its F1value reaches 97.64%. Organization entity has the worst effect. Although the accuracy rate was 73.71%, the recall rate was only 61.11%, which was significantly lower than the former.

The error cases are shown in Table 5. Some labels in organization entity are misjudged as place name labels. For example, "赫章县 (Hezhang)" in the "赫章县民间文学编委会 (Hezhang folk literature Editorial Committee)" is recognized as the place name entity. Combined with the problems of low recall rate and high accuracy of place name entities, it shows that in more cases, organization labels in the original corpus are predicted to be non-organization labels, while the high accuracy shows that non-organization labels in the corpus are rarely predicted to be organization labels. To solve similar problems, it requires the model to strengthen the recognition ability of complex granularity entities on the existing basis (Table 4).

Table 4. Results of various entity types in ENER model.

Model	Precision	Recall	F1 value
LOC	94.57%	88.85%	91.62%
ORG	73.71%	61.11%	66.82%
PER	93.02%	97.97%	95.43%
PRESS	92.19%	96.42%	94.26%
WORK	97.76%	97.52%	97.64%

To further verify the generality of ENER, we compare its F1 values with four excellent methods in recent years [22–25] on Chinese general data sets Resume and MRSA. The former includes 4761 entities, with entity types including nationality (CONT), educational background (EDU), place name (LOC), personal name (name), organizational name (ORG), profession (PRO), race (RACE), and professional title (title). The latter includes 50729 entities, with entity types including place names (LOC), person names (name), and organizational names (ORG) (Table 6).

As shown in Table 7, ENER achieved the best effect on the Resume dataset and the F1 value increased by 1.67% and 0.24% respectively compared with the worst lattice LSTM and the second best MECT. On the MRSA dataset, ENER is slightly inferior to

Table 5. Error Example

Sample text	Reference labels	Real label
赫章县民间文学编委会	B-ORG, I-ORG, I-ORG, I-ORG, I-ORG, I-ORG, I-ORG, I-ORG, I-ORG, I-ORG	B-LOC, I-LOC, I-LOC, I-ORG, I-ORG, I-ORG, I-ORG, I-ORG, I-ORG, I-ORG
秀山民族宗教事务委员会	B-ORG, I-ORG, I-ORG, I-ORG, I-ORG, I-ORG, I-ORG, I-ORG, I-ORG, I-ORG, I-ORG	B-LOC, I-LOC, I-LOC, I-LOC, I-ORG, I-ORG, I-ORG, I-ORG, I-ORG, I-ORG, I-ORG

Table 6. Statistical distribution of entities in Chinese NER datasets.

	Resume	MRSA
Train Set	3821	46364
Validation set	463	-
Test set	477	4365
Total	4761	50729

MECT, but it is higher than the other three models. Compared with most other models, ENER is more stable and has certain scalability.

Table 7. F1 values of different models in public datasets.

Model	Resume	MRSA
Lattice-LSTM	94.46%	93.18%
LR-CNN	95.11%	93.71%
PLTE	95.40%	93.26%
MECT	95.89%	**94.32%**
ENER	**96.13%**	93.85%

To sum up, the ENER model proposed in this paper: (1) based on the BERT pre-training language model, it is superior to the baseline model BiLSTM-CRF in accuracy, recall and F1 value. (2) The context coding layer adopts BiGRU model, which has simple structure and few parameters, and its performance is better than that of BiLSTM on small corpus. (3) The entity boundary detection sub-task is added to improve the entity recognition effect by learning the entity boundary information. (4) Compared with other methods based on deep learning, ENER's performance on the Chinese general data set is also relatively stable. The experimental results show that the ENER model proposed in this paper is effective and extensible in the task of identifying named entities in ethnic ancient books.

5 Conclusion

In this paper, we take the ethnic NER as a case study. The recognition of named entities in the texts of ethnic ancient books is the basis for improving the efficiency of information processing of ancient book inheritance and protection and mining more hidden information. We firstly build a small corpus of ethnic ancient books. Then introduce the boundary detection task into NER model to improve the recognition ability of the model. Experiments on the national ancient books corpus and general data set verify the effectiveness of the method. The next research work will focus on three aspects: (1) Further optimizing the ENER model to improve the performance of ancient book NER tasks; (2) Expand the scope of the corpus and extend the method to a wider range of tasks for extracting entities from ethnic ancient books. (3) Construct the knowledge graph of ethnic ancient books and explore the historical information of Chinese ethnic communication and integration.

References

1. Sundheim, B.: Named entity task definition. In: Proceedings of Message Understanding Conference (1995)
2. Lin, Y., Shen, S.: Neural relation extraction with selective attention over instances. In: Proceedings of the 54th Annual Meeting of the Association for Computational Linguistics, Berlin, Germany, vol. 1, pp. 2124–2133 (2016)
3. Guo, X.: CG-ANER: enhanced contextual embeddings and glyph features-based agricultural named entity recognition. Comput. Electron. Agric. **194**, 106776 (2022)
4. Wu, Z.: Summary of research on named entity recognition technology for electronic medical records. Comput. Eng. Appl. **58**(21), 13–29 (2021)
5. Tong, Z.: Research on military domain named entity recognition based on pre training model. Front. Data Comput. **4**(5), 120–128 (2022)
6. Ma, K.: Ontology-based BERT model for automated information extraction from geological hazard reports. J. Earth Sci. **34**(5), 1390–1405 (2023)
7. Fan, G.: Analysis of hot topics and evolution trends of ancient books digitization research based on Knowledge Mapping. View Publ. **3**(11), 85–87 (2020)
8. Yingjie Wang, F.: A survey of Chinese named entity recognition. J. Front. Comput. Sci. Technol. **17**(2), 324–341 (2023)
9. Liu, C.F., Huang, C.S.: Mining local gazetteers of literary Chinese with CRF and pattern based methods for biographical information in Chinese history. In: 2015 IEEE International Conference on Big Data, Santa Clara, USA, pp. 1629–1638 (2015)
10. Khanam, M.H., Khudhus, M.A., Babu, M.S.P.: Named entity recognition using machine learning techniques for Telugu language. In: 2016 7th IEEE International Conference on Software Engineering and Service Science, Beijing, China, pp. 940–944 (2016)
11. Li, N.: Construction of an automatic extraction model for local chronicles and ancient book aliases based on conditional random fields. J. Chin. Inf. Process. **32**(11), 41–48 (2018)

12. Hinton, G.: Reducing the dimensionality of data with neural networks. Science **313**(5786), 504–507 (2006)
13. Liu, L.: Automatic extraction of traditional musical terms from intangible cultural heritage. Data Anal. Knowl. Disc. **4**(12), 68–75 (2020)
14. Zhao, Z., Zhou, Z., Xing, W., Wu, J., Chang, Y., Li, B.: A neural framework for Chinese medical named entity recognition. In: Xu, R., De, W., Zhong, W., Tian, L., Bai, Y., Zhang, L.-J. (eds.) AIMS 2020. LNCS, vol. 12401, pp. 74–83. Springer, Cham (2020). https://doi.org/10.1007/978-3-030-59605-7_6
15. Lv, H., Ning, Y., Ning, Ke.: ALBERT-based Chinese named entity recognition. In: Yang, Y., Yu, L., Zhang, L.-J. (eds.) ICCC 2020. LNCS, vol. 12408, pp. 79–87. Springer, Cham (2020). https://doi.org/10.1007/978-3-030-59585-2_7
16. Xie, X.: Geological named entity recognition based on BERT and BiGRU-Attention - CRF model. Geol. Bull. China **42**(5), 846–855 (2021)
17. Zhou, F.: Named entity recognition of ancient poems based on Albert-BiLSTM-MHA-CRF model. Wirel. Commun. Mob. Comput. **2022**, 1–11 (2022)
18. Wang, Y.: Geotechnical engineering entity recognition based on BERT-BiGRU-CRF model. Earth Sci. **48**(8), 3137–3150 (2023)
19. Li, X.: Named entity recognition method based on joint entity boundary detection. J. Hebei Univ. Sci. Technol. **44**(1), 20–28 (2023)
20. Chun, C., Kong, F.: Enhancing entity boundary detection for better Chinese named entity recognition. In: Proceedings of the 59th Annual Meeting of the Association for Computational Linguistics and the 11th International Joint Conference on Natural Language Processing, vol. 2, pp. 20–25. Online (2021)
21. Devlin, J.: BERT: pre-training of deep bidirectional transformers for language understanding. arXiv arXiv:1810.04805v1, 11 October 2018
22. Zhang, Y., Yang, J.: Chinese NER using lattice LSTM. In: Proceedings of the 56th Annual Meeting of the Association for Computational Linguistics, Melbourne, Australia, vol. 1, pp. 1554–1564 (2018)
23. Gui, T., Ma, R.: CNN-based Chinese NER with lexicon rethinking. In: Proceedings of the 28th International Joint Conference on Artificial Intelligence, Macao, China, pp. 4982–4988 (2019)
24. Xue, M., Yu, B.: Porous lattice transformer encoder for Chinese NER. In: Proceedings of the 28th International Conference on Computational Linguistics, vol. 1, pp. 3831–3841 (2020). Online
25. Wu, S., Song, X.: MECT: multi-metadata embedding based cross-transformer for Chinese named entity recognition. In: Proceedings of the 59th Annual Meeting of the Association for Computational Linguistics and the 11th International Joint Conference on Natural Language Processing, vol. 1, pp. 1529–1539 (2021). Online

An Enhanced Opposition-Based Golden-Sine Whale Optimization Algorithm

Yong Lu[✉], Chao Yi, Jiayun Li, and Wentao Li

School of Information Engineering, Minzu University of China, Beijing, China
22301996@muc.edu.cn

Abstract. The Whale Optimization Algorithm is an ingenious method conceived by researchers, drawing inspiration from the feeding behavior of humpback whales. Characterized by its simple structure, limited parameters, high efficiency, and robust optimization capacity, WOA has been extensively applied across multiple domains to address various challenges. Nonetheless, it has been found that the algorithm demonstrates low global exploration capability, inadequate search precision, and susceptibility to local optima entrapment. Many enhancements have been suggested in the literature, with Opposition-Based Learning emerging as a particularly effective technique for improving the quality of the initial population. In the present study, we put forth the Enhanced Opposition-Based strategy, which integrates supplementary constraints into the existing Opposition-Based Learning framework, generating a more refined initial population. Furthermore, we introduce the Golden Sine Algorithm to modify the optimization approach of WOA, fostering an equilibrium between global exploration and exploitation abilities. In our evaluation, the proposed algorithm is assessed on nine classic benchmark functions with a dimensionality of 500, and compared with the original WOA, An enhanced whale optimization algorithm (eWOA), and the Elite Opposition-Based Golden-Sine Whale Optimization Algorithm (EGolden-SWOA). The results exemplify the superior performance of our proposed algorithm, underscoring its potential application in the optimization of truss structure design problems, the results indicate that ESWOA outperforms other enhanced algorithms, such as eWOA and EGolden-SWOA, in terms of its performance in engineering optimization. This signifies that ESWOA can be effectively applied to engineering optimization problems.

Keywords: Whale optimization algorithm · Opposition-Based Learning · Golden Sine algorithm · engineering optimization

1 Introduction

Inspired by various natural phenomena, swarm intelligence algorithms seek efficient solutions for complex real-world problems by simulating mechanisms such as biological evolution, collective behavior, or neural networks. Due to their strong adaptability and robustness, swarm-based optimization algorithms have found wide applications in fields such as civil engineering, mechanical engineering, electrical engineering, machine learning, neural network optimization, aerospace engineering design, signal processing, and more. Meta-heuristics (MH), predominantly emulating physical or biological behaviors in nature, are known for their stochastic nature, enabling them to effectively avoid local optima. Additionally, they possess characteristics of simplicity, flexibility, stability, and efficiency, making them applicable across diverse domains. Particle Swarm Optimization (PSO) [1], Artificial Bee Colony (ABC) [2], Firefly Algorithm (FA) [3], Selfish Herd Optimizer (SHO) [4], Bat Algorithm (BA) [5], Krill-Herd (KH) [6], Grey Wolf Optimizer (GWO) [7], and Whale Optimization Algorithm (WOA) [8] are typical examples of MH algorithms. These algorithms begin with a set of randomly chosen solutions and aim to enhance the quality of these solutions based on a fitness function. By repeatedly perturbing the existing solutions according to a set of simple rules, the algorithms augment the value of the fitness function. The key challenge in MH lies in balancing the global search ability and local exploitation capability. The global exploration phase aims to search the target space as extensively as possible, with a well-executed global search helping to prevent the occurrence of local optima problems. On the other hand, the local exploitation phase involves developing promising regions in hopes of obtaining better solutions.

Additionally, the quality of initial solutions is also a crucial consideration in MH algorithms. Numerous researchers have utilized chaotic maps to improve MH algorithms and aid in finding superior initial solutions. Apart from the chaotic map strategy, another popular strategy known as opposition-based learning (OBL) [9] has been employed to enhance the quality of initial solutions for most swarm algorithms. The primary approach of OBL is to generate "opposite" local solutions in the initial or optimization stages to improve the algorithm's exploratory behavior and enhance the quality of initial solutions. Based on the characteristics of the OBL strategy, Alamri et al. proposed a modified version of WOA using the OBL strategy [10]. Elaziz et al. [11] presented the OBL-based WOA strategy to generate the initial population and during the updating stage of the solution. This algorithm was applied to find the optimal parameter values for a solar diode model.

WOA, proposed by Mirjalili et al. [8] in 2016, is a novel meta-heuristic algorithm inspired by the hunting behavior of humpback whales in nature. Based on a biological model, WOA facilitates global search and local exploitation in large-scale, high-dimensional complex problems. It leverages the characteristics of whale hunting, enabling efficient search in the global space and precise locking onto high-quality solutions. WOA has attracted widespread attention due to its minimal parameter settings, high efficiency, and strong optimization capabilities. However, it also has limitations, such as weak global exploration ability, slow convergence speed, and susceptibility to local optima.

In this paper, we propose improvements to OBL strategy. By introducing certain constraints on the generation of opposition solutions in the initial population, a new initial population is obtained. Some individuals with the best fitness from the three populations are selected to achieve a more diverse and higher quality initial population. Additionally, we introduce the Golden Sine Algorithm (Golden-SA) [12] to optimize the global search ability of whales, achieving a better balance between global exploration and local exploitation.

The main contributions of this paper are as follows: (1) Improvement of the OBL strategy to enhance the diversity and quality of the initial population. (2) Integration of the enhanced OBL with Golden-SA and application to engineering optimization problems.

The remaining structure of this paper is organized as follows: Sect. 2 introduces related work. Section 3 presents the basic WOA algorithm. A detailed description of the proposed algorithm is presented in Sect. 4. Section 5 conducts experimental simulations and compares the proposed algorithm with three other algorithms. Section 6 discusses the application of the algorithm in engineering. Section 7 summarizes the advantages and disadvantages of the algorithm and provides prospects for future development.

2 Related Work

WOA, a type of collective intelligent metaheuristic, was inspired by the predatory behavior of humpback whales. It was initially proposed by scholar Mirjalili et al. [8] and has since gained extensive attention due to its low parameter settings, high efficiency, and strong optimization capabilities. However, despite its efficiency, WOA lacks global exploration abilities, often exhibiting slow convergence speeds and a tendency to get trapped in local optima. As a result, numerous researchers have conducted various improvements on WOA. The Hybrid Whale-PSO Algorithm (HWPSO), proposed by Laskar et al. [13], is a novel population-based hybrid metaheuristic algorithm designed to tackle complex optimization problems. By combining PSO and WOA, this algorithm overcomes the limitations associated with the exploration phase of PSO. Introducing WOA during the global exploration phase of PSO effectively prevents PSO from getting trapped in local optima. Moreover, during the development phase of WOA, PSO can impose constraints on the random search mechanism of WOA. Simulation results demonstrate that HWPSO performs remarkably well in terms of optimization performance. Ling et al. [14] made improvements to WOA by incorporating Levy flight trajectories, which enhanced its global exploration capabilities and reduced the likelihood of getting trapped in local optima. Bozorgi et al. [15] proposed the improved whale optimization algorithm (IWOA) and IWOA +, where they utilized Differential Evolution (DE) to enhance the global exploration capabilities of WOA. Elaziz et al.[16] introduced the differential evolution-based WOA with a chaotic map and opposition-based learning (DEWCO). They selected an effective chaotic map from various chaotic maps using DE, resulting in promising results. Ding et al. [17] proposed the theories of chaos initialization, nonlinear convergence factor, and chaotic inertia weight to balance the global exploration and exploitation abilities of WOA. Tanyildizi et al. [12] introduced the Golden Sine Algorithm (Golden-SA) in 2017. It is a novel intelligent algorithm characterized by its rapid convergence, robustness, and ease of implementation.

Xiao et al. [18] proposed another variant of WOA called the Elite Opposition-Based Golden-Sine Whale Optimization Algorithm (EGolden-SWOA). This algorithm employs the Elite Opposition-Based strategy to enhance the diversity and quality of the initial population, effectively improving the algorithm's convergence speed. The introduction of Golden Section optimization optimizes the search strategy of WOA, thereby balancing the algorithm's global exploration and local exploitation capabilities. Experimental results demonstrate its favorable performance. Chakraborty et al.

[19] introduced an enhanced Whale Optimization Algorithm (eWOA). This algorithm introduces a selection parameter to replace the convergence factor, balancing the global exploration and local exploitation capabilities of the algorithm. The coefficients A and C are modified, and random movement during the exploration phase is allowed. Moreover, an inertia weight is introduced. Experimental results prove that eWOA exhibits better performance when handling high-dimensional problems.

From the above discussions, it can be observed that, like other metaheuristic algorithms, the key points of WOA lie in balancing the trade-off between global exploration and local exploitation, as well as enhancing the quality of the initial population. Based on this observation, this paper introduces a novel enhanced WOA. By employing the Enhanced Opposition-Based strategy, this algorithm effectively enhances the diversity and quality of the initial solutions, laying a solid foundation for subsequent iterations and improving the convergence speed of the algorithm. Additionally, Golden Section optimization is introduced to optimize the search strategy of WOA, harmonizing its global search capability and development capability.

3 Whale Optimization Algorithm

Whales, as intelligent creatures in the ocean, possess astonishing cognitive abilities. They exhibit highly complex social behavior and learning capabilities, making them important subjects of study in marine biology and animal behavior research. Whales are exceptionally intelligent, with intellectual capacities comparable to those of several-year-old children. WOA is inspired by the hunting behavior of sperm whales, which primarily uses the bubble-net foraging method. Mirjalili et al. designed the WOA based on the predatory behavior of sperm whales.

The basic process of the WOA is as follows: assuming that there are n whales distributed in a d-dimensional space, the position of the i-th whale in the t-th generation is denoted as $X_i^t = (X_{i,1}, X_{i,2}, \ldots, X_{i,d})$, $(i = 1, 2, \ldots, n; t = 1, 2, \ldots, T)$ T represents the maximum number of iterations, and the global best position, representing the prey's location, is denoted as $X_{best}^t = (X_{best,1}, X_{best,2}, \ldots, X_{best,d})$.

Since the initial whale population does not have a prey location, it is initialized using the current best positions of the whales, and the other whales employ different strategies to approach the prey location. In the WOA, there are three ways to update the positions of the whales.

3.1 Searching the Prey

Whales can exchange position information with other individuals in the population. Each whale randomly selects another whale and swims towards its position. The position update process is as follows:

$$X_i^{t+1} = X_{rand}^t - A * D_1 \tag{1}$$

where X_{rand}^t represents the position of the randomly selected whale from the current population, $D_1 = C * X_{rand}^t - X_i^t$ represents the distance between the individual X_i^t and the randomly selected whale position X_{rand}^t. The parameter C is defined as $C = 2 * r_1$ and parameter A is defined as $A = 2a * r_2 - a$, where r_1 and r_2 are random numbers between 0 and 1, $a = 2 - \frac{2*t}{T}$ is the convergence factor that linearly decreases from 2 to 0 during the iterative process. C is a random number between 0 and 2 and dynamically affects the size of the random whale's influence on the current whale's position. A larger value of C corresponds to a stronger influence, while a smaller value corresponds to a weaker influence.

3.2 Encircling the Prey

Whales can identify the position of the prey (optimal function value) and surround it. The position update formula for this process is as follows:

$$X_i^{t+1} = X_{best}^t - A * D_2 \tag{2}$$

where $D_2 = \left| C * X_{best}^t - X_i^t \right|$, represents the distance between X_i^t and the global best position X_{best}^t. C controls the degree of influence between the prey position and the current individual, with a larger C resulting in a stronger influence.

3.3 Bubble-net Attacking Strategy

Whales move towards the prey direction and attack it using a spiral motion known as bubble-net foraging. The position update formula for this hunting process is as follows:

$$X_i^{t+1} = D_3 * e^{bl} * \cos(2\pi l) + X_{best}^t \tag{3}$$

where $D_3 = \left| X_{best}^t - X_i^t \right|$, represents the distance between the individual and the prey, and the shape of the spiral is determined by a constant l, which is a random number between -1 and 1. Whales swim around the prey, continuously spewing bubbles in a spiral motion to shrink the range. Assuming that the probability of whales choosing either surrounding hunting or bubble-net hunting is equal, this behavior can be represented as follows:

$$X_i^{t+1} = \begin{cases} X_{best}^t - A * D, & p < 0.5 \\ D_3 * e^{bl} * \cos(2\pi l) + X_{best}^t, & p \geq 0.5 \end{cases} \tag{4}$$

When $|A| < 1$, the individual whale surrounds the prey and moves towards the prey direction. When $|A| >= 1$, the individual whale searches for the prey and deviates from its position to find a better individual. Therefore, the value of parameter A determines whether the whale performs the position update according to Eq. (1) or Eq. (4). The magnitude of parameter A largely depends on the value of the convergence factor a, making a an important factor in balancing the algorithm's exploration and exploitation.

WOA has several advantages, such as a simple structure, minimal parameters, high efficiency, and robust optimisation capabilities. However, WOA's random initial population can produce poor quality initial solutions, which reduces both the convergence rate and the accuracy of the algorithm. In the bubble net attack strategy, the whales move forward in a spiral motion guided by the location of their prey, which promotes faster convergence but can also lead to trapping in local optima. Consequently, to address these shortcomings, this paper proposes An Enhanced Opposition-Based Golden-Sine Whale Optimization Algorithm.

4 Enhanced Opposition-Based Golden-Sine Whale Optimization Algorithm

4.1 Enhanced Opposition-Based

OBL was first introduced by Tizhoosh in 2005 [8], and has since been employed to ameliorate the performance of numerous swarm algorithms. OBL is particularly efficacious in augmenting the diversity and quality of the population while circumventing the premature convergence into a local optimum state. The principal methodology of OBL entails generating an antithetical solution to the current one during the initialization phase, and subsequently selecting the optimal solution between the existing and antithetical solutions to engender the new generation of individuals. This process can substantively bolster the algorithm's exploration capacity. In the instance of WOA, the initial population is generated stochastically, thereby precluding the assurance of the initial population's quality. To enhance WOA's global exploration capabilities and refine the initial population's quality, we propose a novel dual-inverse learning strategy predicated upon the quadratic-inverse learning strategy developed by Meng et al. [20]. The specific concepts are delineated as follows:

Definition 1 (Opposite Solution): Presuming that a viable solution of the current population is $X = (x_1, x_2, \ldots, x_d)(x_i \in [ub_j, lb_j])$, its corresponding opposite solution can be represented as $\overline{X} = (\overline{x_1}, \overline{x_2}, \ldots, \overline{x_d})$, where in $\overline{X_j} = \omega(ub_j + lb_j) - X_j$, with ω being a generalized coefficient uniformly distributed within the range of [0,1].

Definition 2 (Enhanced Opposition Solution): Assuming that an individual of the present population is $X_{i,j} = (x_{i,1}, x_{i,2}, \ldots, x_{i,d})$, its respective opposite solution is $\overline{X_{i,j}} = (\overline{x_{i,1}}, \overline{x_{i,2}}, \ldots, \overline{x_{i,d}})$, which can be expressed as:

$$\overline{X_{i,j}} = k(a_j + b_j) - X_{i,j} \tag{5}$$

where k is a dynamic coefficient confined within the interval [0,1], $a_j = \min(X_{i,j}), b_j = \max(X_{i,j})$, and a_j and b_j serve as dynamic boundaries. If this operation causes $X_{i,j}$ to surpass the boundary and become an infeasible solution, then the solution can be reestablished by employing the following method:

$$\overline{X_{i,j}} = rand(a_j, b_j) \tag{6}$$

Subsequently, the enhanced opposite solution can be defined as:

$$X_{i,j}^o = rand[X^o, X_{i,j}] \tag{7}$$

where $X^o = \mu * (a_j + b_j), \mu = \theta * \frac{2}{3}$, and θ constitutes a random value within the range of [0,1].

4.2 Golden Sine Algorithm

Golden-SA, a novel intelligent optimization technique, was first introduced by Erkan Tanyildizi in 2017 [14]. Drawing inspiration from the sine function in mathematics, Golden-SA exhibits attributes such as swift convergence, robust performance, and straightforward implementation. In 2019, Xiao et al. [18]successfully applied Golden-SA to WOA and obtained favorable outcomes. The position update formula for Golden-SA is as follows:

$$X_i^{t+1} = X_i^t * |sin(r_3)| + r_4 * sin(r_3) * |\alpha_1 * X_{Best}^t - \alpha_2 * X_I^t| \qquad (8)$$

In this equation, X_i^{t+1} denotes the position of the ith individual within d-dimensional space at the $(t + 1)$th iteration, while X_{Best}^t corresponds to the optimal position of individual i during the tth iteration. Furthermore, the random value r_3, which falls within the interval $[0, 2\pi]$, dictates the distance of individual movement for the subsequent iteration. The random value r_4, ranging between $[0, \pi]$, specifies the direction of the position update for individual i at the next iteration. Lastly, $\alpha_1 = -\pi + \left(1 - \frac{\sqrt{5}-1}{2}\right)$, $\alpha_2 = -\pi + 2\pi * \frac{\sqrt{5}-1}{2}$.

4.3 Enhanced Opposition-Based Golden-Sine Whale Optimization Algorithm

In response to the numerous limitations of WOA, this paper introduces the Enhanced Opposition-Based Golden-Sine Whale Optimization Algorithm. The Enhanced Opposition-Based strategy is implemented to amplify the diversity and quality of the initial population. By ranking the random, opposition, and enhanced populations based on their fitness values, the optimal individuals can be chosen, thereby significantly improving the initial population's diversity and quality while circumventing local optima. For each generation of the population, OBL generates opposite solutions to escape the initial populations that may produce local solutions. Enhanced Opposition learning adds randomness grounded on the reverse solutions, consequently boosting the algorithm's local search capabilities. Moreover, the dynamic boundary tracking search technique within the reinforced opposition learning enables the initial population to shrink spatially, fostering the algorithm's global convergence potential.

This paper builds upon the study by Xiao et al., titled "Study on Enhanced Opposition-Based Golden-Sine Whale Optimization Algorithm (EGolden—SWOA)", maintaining the enclosure hunting and random hunting strategies of the fundamental WOA while refining the Bubble-net attacking strategy using Golden-SA. The Bubble-net attacking strategy directs whales to spiral forward towards the current best prey's position. Although this method accelerates the algorithm's convergence rate, it drastically reduces population diversity and increases the propensity for falling into local optima. Addressing this issue, this paper enhances the Bubble-net attacking strategy employing Golden-SA. In each iteration, whale individuals exchange information with the best individual while parameters r_3 and r_4 govern the position update distance and direction. This optimization advances the basic WOA algorithm's search process, steadily guiding individuals towards the ultimate value and harmonizing the algorithm's global exploration and local exploitation capabilities. Consequently, this optimizes the algorithm's accuracy and speed.

The specific steps for implementing the Enhanced Reverse Learning Golden-Sine Whale Optimization Algorithm are as follows:

1. Establish relevant parameters.
2. Initialize the population, encompassing the number of individuals P, dimensionality of candidate solutions d, and maximum number of iterations T.
3. Determine the current boundaries using $a_j = \min(X_{i,j})$ and $b_j = \max(X_{i,j})$.
4. Update the optimal position and optimal value.
5. For each individual in the population, generate reverse solutions with Eq. (5) and enhanced reverse solutions using Eq. (7).
6. Arrange the current population, reverse population, and enhanced reverse population based on objective function fitness values. Choose the best P populations for the subsequent generation and mark the most suitable individual as prey.
7. Refresh parameters a, A, and C.
8. If $|A| \geq 1$, locate the prey employing Eq. (1).
9. If $|A| < 1$, surround the prey using Eq. (4).
10. Examine whether the new position surpasses the boundaries. If not, update the position; if so, assign it to the boundary value.
11. Iterate steps 3 to 10 until reaching the maximum number of iterations.

Figure 1. shows the ESWOA algorithm flowchart.

5 Numerical Results and Discussion

5.1 Benchmark Function

To further ascertain the global optimization and developmental capabilities of ESWOA in comparison with other advanced Whale Optimization Algorithms, this study selects the following for comparative analysis: the basic WOA, the enhanced whale optimization algorithm (eWOA), the Elite Reverse Learning Golden-Sine Whale Optimization Algorithm (EGolden-SWOA), and ESWOA. The population size for all algorithms is set to 30, and the number of iterations is set to 500. All common parameters are maintained consistent. The specific information for the Benchmark functions is shown in Table 1.

5.2 Comparative Analysis with other Intelligent Algorithms

To validate the rationality and effectiveness of the proposed ESWOA algorithm, this study conducts experiments on the algorithm's performance using multiple benchmark functions. To mitigate randomness, the ESWOA algorithm is independently executed 30 times on each benchmark function and compared with the other three algorithms. The experimental results are shown in Table 2.

Functions f_1 to f_6 are unimodal benchmark functions frequently employed to evaluate the developmental capabilities of the algorithm. Based on the experimental results, for f_1, the EGolden-SWOA algorithm achieves superior optimization effects, reaching the optimal value of 0. In comparison to EGolden-SWOA, the average optimization effect of ESWOA can also attain an optimal value of 0. ESWOA evidently exhibits

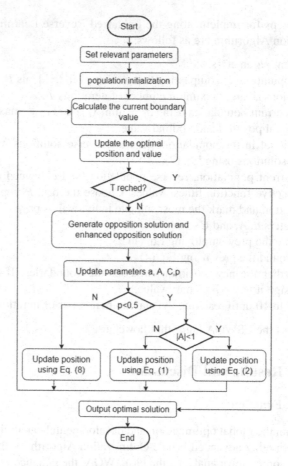

Fig. 1. ESWOA algorithm flowchart.

significantly enhanced optimization capabilities in contrast to EGolden-SWOA, with improved versions of WOA performing substantially stronger than the WOA. For f_2, both EGolden-SWOA and ESWOA algorithms present an optimal value of 0; however, ESWOA outperforms EGolden-SWOA regarding their average values. Generally, eWOA excels in all aspects in comparison to WOA but is not as effective as ESWOA and EGolden-SWOA. For f_3, the average value of ESWOA can reach the optimal value of 0, performing better than EGolden-SWOA. The WOA exhibits the lowest performance. For f_4 and f_5, the overall effect of ESWOA is marginally superior to EGolden-SWOA, albeit the optimization effects of all four algorithms for these two functions are suboptimal. For f_6, ESWOA significantly outperforms EGolden-SWOA in all aspects. The optimization impact of eWOA is weaker than the first two, yet stronger than the WOA. Overall, regarding the developmental capabilities of the algorithm, the improved versions of WOA are substantially more robust than WOA, with eWOA demonstrating a markedly improved performance relative to WOA and EGolden-SWOA exhibiting superior overall performance compared to eWOA. ESWOA manifests the most exceptional

Table 1. Benchmark function information.

Benchmark function	D	Range	Min
$f_1 = \sum_{i=1}^{n} x_i^2$	30	[-100,100]	0
$f_2 = \sum_{i=1}^{n} \left(\sum_{j=1}^{i} x_j \right)^2$	30	[-100,100]	0
$f_3 = \sum_{i=1}^{n} i x_i^2$	30	[-10,10]	0
$f_4 = \sum_{i=1}^{n-1} \left[100(x_{i+1} - x_i^2)^2 + (x_i - 1)^2 \right]$	30	[-30,30]	0
$f_5 = \sum_{i=1}^{n} (\lfloor x_i + 0.5 \rfloor)^2$	30	[-100,100]	0
$f_6 = \max\{|x_i|, 1 \le i \le n\}$	30	[-100,100]	0
$f_7 = \sum_{i=1}^{11} \left[a_i - \dfrac{x_1(b_i^2 + b_i x_2)}{b_i^2 + b_i x_3 + x_4} \right]^2$	30	[-5,5]	0.00030
$f_8 = -20\exp\left(-0.2\sqrt{\dfrac{1}{n}\sum_{i=1}^{n} x_i^2} \right)$ $- \exp\left(\dfrac{1}{n}\sum_{i=1}^{n} \cos(2\pi x_i) \right) + 20 + e$	30	[-32,32]	0
$f_9 = \left[1 + (x_1 + x_2 + 1)^2 (19 - 14x_1 + 3x_1^2 - 14x_2 + 6x_1 x_2 + 3x_2^2) \right]$ $* \left[30 + (2x_1 - 3x_2)^2 * (18 - 32x_1 + 12x_1^2 + 48x_2 - 36x_1 x_2 + 27x_2^2) \right]$	30	[-2,2]	3

Table 2. Benchmark function experimental results.

		WOA	eWOA	EGolden -SWOA	ESWOA
f_1	Best	1.10E-100	0	0	0
	Mean	2.99E-69	7.19E-206	6.32E-279	0
	SD	1.61E-68	0	0	0
f_2	Best	2.59E + 00	0	0	0
	Mean	3.74E + 00	6.41E-111	1.71E-223	6.03E-269
	SD	8.88E + 00	3.45E-110	0	0
f_3	Best	1.37E-258	0	0	0
	Mean	9.07E-63	1.64E-212	1.75E-280	0
	SD	4.88E-62	0	0	0
f_4	Best	2.56E-01	1.40E-03	2.72E-09	2.75E-10
	Mean	2.55E + 00	1.03E + 00	2.57E-07	2.46E-09
	SD	0.9471E + 00	5.14E + 00	9.16E-02	9.04E-01
f_5	Best	7.43 E-01	2.75 E-21	3.76 E-09	2.72 E-11
	Mean	1.12E-01	1.15 E-09	2.39E-08	8.93 E-10
	SD	2.60E-01	6.21 E-09	1.28 E-07	0
f_6	Best	7.43E-03	2.75E-271	3.76E-204	2.72E-245
	Mean	1.12E + 00	1.15E-90	2.39E-141	8.93E-172
	SD	2.60E + 00	6.21E-90	1.28E-140	0
f_7	Best	0.0003	0.0003	0.0003	0.0003
	Mean	0.0006	0.0004	0.0003	0.0003
	SD	1.25E-04	7.13E-04	6.58E-05	4.65E-05
f_8	Best	7.54E-15	4.44E-16	4.44E-16	4.44E-16
	Mean	7.54E-15	4.44E-16	4.44E-16	4.44E-16
	SD	0	0	0	0
f_9	Best	3.00	3.00	3.00	3.00
	Mean	3.00	3.00	3.00	3.00
	SD	5.39E-7	1.03E-3	1.13E-5	5.41E-4

overall performance in all aspects, with a standard deviation of 0 for F1, F2, F5, F6, and F7, indicating robust optimization stability for ESWOA.

Functions f_7 to f_9 are multimodal benchmark functions typically utilized to test the algorithm's global exploration capabilities. According to the experimental findings, for f_7, the average values of ESWOA and EGolden-SWOA surpass the other two functions. For f_8, the improved versions of WOA exhibit marginally superior performance to WOA.

In general, the overall global optimization capabilities of ESWOA are more advanced than WOA, eWOA, and EGolden-SWOA.

To further corroborate the convergence performance of ESWOA, this study delineates convergence graphs for several benchmark functions (f_1, f_3, f_6, and f_8). The x-axis represents the number of iterations, and the y-axis denotes the logarithmically transformed fitness values.

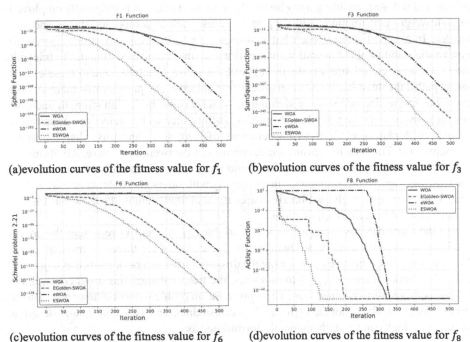

(a)evolution curves of the fitness value for f_1 (b)evolution curves of the fitness value for f_3

(c)evolution curves of the fitness value for f_6 (d)evolution curves of the fitness value for f_8

Fig. 2. Evolution curve of fitness values for some benchmark functions.

As observed in Fig. 2(d), the Enhanced Opposition-Based strategy significantly ameliorates the quality of the initial population, paving the way for expeditious iteration of the population. As seen in Fig. 2(a), the utilization of the Golden-Sine function results in a more rapid convergence speed for both EGolden-SWOA and ESWOA. Nonetheless, it is evident that the Enhanced Opposition-Based strategy procures more improved initial population values and therefore leads to a faster convergence rate. As noted in Fig. 2(c), ESWOA displays superior capability in escaping local optima during the intermediate stages of iterations compared to other functions. Whether a unimodal or multimodal function, the Enhanced Opposition-Based strategy provides an excellent initial population, resulting in a rapid convergence rate. This fully demonstrates the significant improvement of the Enhanced Opposition-Based strategy for WOA and its capacity to augment the performance of WOA.

6 Engineering Optimization Application of ESWOA

This paper implements ESWOA to address engineering optimization problems and demonstrates its superior performance in comparison to WOA, eWOA, and EGolden-SWOA.

The three-bar truss is a basic truss structure comprising three linear bars interconnected to form a stable triangle. This structure exhibits exceptional mechanical performance and stiffness, enabling it to effectively withstand loads. It is frequently employed in lightweight constructions and support systems, such as temporary stages and sun shades. In a three-bar truss, each bar is responsible for bearing a portion of stress to ensure the stability of the overall structure. Bars are interconnected at nodes to transmit stress, creating closed stress paths throughout the entire structure. Due to these closed stress paths, the three-bar truss can endure external loads. The primary raw materials for three-bar trusses include steel or aluminum, which exhibit both high strength and corrosion resistance. During the design process, factors such as bar selection, dimensions (diameter, thickness, etc.), and considerations of load, span, and truss shape must be accounted for. These factors ensure the rationality of the overall structure. Additionally, connection methods like welding, bolting, and riveting are commonly employed to join the bars together. These components must comply with safety and stability requirements. Due to its simplicity, high load-bearing capacity, and light weight, the three-bar truss is widely utilized in various applications.

In the three-bar truss design problem, variables x_1, x_2, and x_3 represent the cross-sectional areas of the three bars. Owing to the symmetry of the three-bar truss, $x_1 = x_3$. Consequently, the objective of designing the three-bar truss can be described as adjusting the cross-sectional areas (x_1, x_1) to minimize the truss volume. The stress constraint ε is applied to each truss component. This optimization problem encompasses a nonlinear fitness function, three nonlinear inequality constraints, and two continuous decision variables, which can be mathematically formulated as:

$$\min f(x) = \left(2\sqrt{2}x_1 + x_2\right) * l \tag{9}$$

Constraints:

$$g_1(x) = \frac{\sqrt{2}x_1 + x_2}{\sqrt{2}x_1^2 + 2x_1 x_2} * p - \varepsilon \leq 0 \tag{10}$$

$$g_2(x) = \frac{x_2}{\left(\sqrt{2}x_1^2 + 2x_1 x_2\right)} * p - \varepsilon \leq 0 \tag{11}$$

$$g_3(x) = \frac{1}{\left(\sqrt{2}x_2 + x_1\right)} * p - \varepsilon \leq 0 \tag{12}$$

where $l = 100\,\text{cm}$, $p = 2kN/\text{cm}^2$, $\varepsilon = 2kN/\text{cm}^2$.

The basic WOA, eWOA, EGolden-SWOA, and ESWOA algorithms are employed to solve this problem. All four algorithms share identical parameter settings, with the results displayed in Table 3. It can be observed that for the three-bar truss design problem, both EGolden-SWOA and ESWOA achieve the optimal value of 271.50, while WOA and eWOA exhibit marginally lower solution accuracy and stability. EGolden-SWOA and

ESWOA demonstrate higher solution accuracy and stability compared to the other two algorithms. ESWOA possesses greater stability than EGolden-SWOA. Thus, ESWOA can be effectively applied to engineering optimization problems.

Table 3. Solution results for the three-bar truss design problem.

algorithm	Best	Mean	SD
WOA	271.54	275.58	30.23
eWOA	271.51	275.54	11.75
EGolden—SWOA	271.50	271.50	0.53
ESWOA	271.50	271.50	0.03

7 Conclusion

This paper introduces an Enhanced Opposition-Based strategy that effectively enhances the diversity and quality of WOA's initial population, providing a superior foundation for subsequent iterations. In conjunction with the Golden-SA algorithm, this strategy alters the optimization method of WOA, enabling the algorithm to better balance global exploration and local exploitation. Evaluations of nine classic benchmark functions are conducted, and the results are compared with the three algorithms, substantiating the effectiveness of ESWOA in engineering optimization. This research augments the quality of the initial population, optimally balances the relationship between exploration and exploitation, and improves WOA's performance. However, this study also has limitations. In future work, it is hoped that the quality of the population can be further enhanced and the exploration-exploitation balance can be more comprehensively investigated. The algorithm should also be extended to a broader range of domains.

References

1. Kennedy, J., Eberhart, R.C.: Particle swarm optimization, In: Proceedings of the IEEE International Conference on Neural Networks, pp. 1942–1948 (1995)
2. Karaboga, D.: An idea based on honeybee swarm for numerical optimization, Technical Report TR06. Erciyes University, Engineering Faculty, Computer Engineering Department (2005)
3. Yang, X.S.: Nature-Inspired Meta-heuristic Algorithms, Luniver Press (2008)
4. Fausto, F., Cuevas, E., Valdivia, A., Gonzalez, A.: A global optimization algorithm inspired in the behavior of selfish herds. Biosystems **160**, 39–55 (2017)
5. Hasançebi, O., Teke, T., Pekcan, O.: A bat-inspired algorithm for structural optimization. Comput. Struct. **128**, 77–90 (2013)
6. Gandomi, A.H., Alavi, A.H.: S, pp. 335–349. Talatahari, Structural Optimization Using Krill Herd Algorithm, Swarm Intelligence and Bio-Inspired Computation (2013)
7. Mirjalili, S., Mirjalili, S.M.: Andrew Lewis, Grey Wolf Optimizer. Adv. Eng. Softw. **69**, 46–61 (2014)

8. Mirjalili, S., Lewis, A.: The whale optimization algorithm. Adv. Eng. Softw. **95**, 5167 (2016)
9. Tizhoosh, H.R.: 0pposition—based learning: a new scheme for machine intelligence[A]. In: International Conference on Computational Intelligence for Modelling, Control and Automation, 2005 and International Conference on Intelligent Agents, Web Technologies and Internet Commerce[C]. Vienna, Austria: IEEE, pp. 695—701 (2005)
10. Alamri, H.S., Alsariera, Y.A., Kamal, Z., et al., Opposition-based Whale Optimization Algorithm. Faculty of Computer System & Software Engineering (2017)
11. Elaziz, M.A., Oliva, D.: Parameter estimation of solar cells diode models by an improved opposition-based whale optimization algorithm. Energy Convers. Manage. **171**, 1843–1859 (2018)
12. Tanyildizi, E., Demir, G.: Golden sine algorithm: a novel math—inspired algorithm. Adv. E1ectrical Comput. Eng. **17**(2), 71—78 (2017)
13. Laskar, N.M., Guha, K., Chatterjee, I., Chanda, S., Baishnab, K.L., Paul, P.K.: HWPSO: a new hybrid whale-particle swarm optimization algorithm and its application in electronic design optimization problems. Appl. Intell. pp. 1–27 (2018)
14. Ling, Y., Zhou, Y., Luo, Q.: Lévy flight trajectory-based whale optimization algorithm for global optimization. IEEE Access **5**, 6168–6186 (2017)
15. Mostafa Bozorgi, S., Yazdani, S.: IWOA: an improved whale optimization algorithm for optimization problems, J. Comput. Des. Eng. **6**(3) 243–259 (2019)
16. Abd Elaziz, M., Mirjalili, S.: A hyper-heuristic for improving the initial population of whale optimization algorithm. Knowl.-Based Syst. **172,** 42–63 (2019)
17. Ding, H., Wu, Z., Zhao, L.: Whale optimization algorithm based on nonlinear convergence factor and chaotic inertial weight, Concurr. Comput.: Pract. Exper. **32**(24), e5949 (2020)
18. Xiao, Z.: Study on elite opposition—based golden-sine whale optimization algorithm and its application of project optimization. Acta Electron. Sin. **47**(10), 2177–2186 (2019)
19. Chakraborty, S., Saha, A.K., Chakraborty, R.: An enhanced whale optimization algorithm for large scale optimization problems, Knowl.-Based Syst. **233**, 107543 (2021)
20. Meng, L.: An improved estimation of distribution algorithm with extreme elitism selection and opposition -based learning. Comput. Simul. **38**(1), 236–241 (2021)

T4S: Two-Stage Screenplay Synopsis Summary Generation with Turning Points

Depei Wang[1,2], Wenyi Sun[3], Cheng Luo[1], Dachang Liu[1], Ruibin Mao[4], and Ruifeng Xu[2(✉)]

[1] Guangdong Southern Planning & Designing Institute of Telecom Co., Ltd, Shenzhen 518063, China
wangdepei@spid.com.cn, {luocheng,liudc}@spdi.com.cn
[2] Harbin Institute of Technology (Shenzhen), Shenzhen 518055, China
xuruifeng@hit.edu.cn
[3] Hubei University, Wuhan 430062, China
swy_11202020@163.com
[4] Shenzhen Securities Information Co., Ltd, Shenzhen 518010, China
maoruibin@cninfo.com.cn

Abstract. The recent advancements in neural network models and the availability of vast amounts of data, automatic summarization technology has become one of the primary solutions for dealing with information overload and pinpointing key information. Unlike narrative text, movie scripts consist of sequences of scene descriptions, and directly compressing the text may lead to truncation of plot-relevant content. Furthermore, movie script summarization tasks lack datasets that align script content with plot summaries. Therefore, this paper proposes a two-stage method T4S for generating plot summaries of movie scripts. First, the GraphTP model is employed as an extractor to extract key turning scenes from the scene text sequences. Second, an unsupervised text matching method is used to obtain text pairs that match scenes with plot summaries. Finally, a generator, utilizing an efficiently fine-tuned LLM, rewrites key scene text and concatenates it to form the final plot summary of the movie script. The results of the implementation show that the proposed method in this paper outperforms baseline methods.

Keywords: Abstractive Summarization · Semantic Matching · Data Mining · Natural Language Processing

1 Introduction

Movie script is typical examples of long text, comprised of a series of scene descriptions and dialogues. Using text summarization technique to convert screenplay into concise plot summary is one of the essential methods for understanding and identifying key information within the script. Text summarization techniques are typically categorized into extractive summarization and abstractive summarization based on how the model compresses the text [14]. In extractive summarization [3], text is summarized by selecting and extracting the most

X. Pan et al. (Eds.): ICCC 2023, LNCS 14207, pp. 75–86, 2024.
https://doi.org/10.1007/978-3-031-51671-9_6

important original content based on a scoring mechanism. Abstractive summarization [16], on the other hand, involves a deeper understanding of the original text and rephrasing it without altering its main meaning. Common strategies for summarizing long texts, like movie scripts, often involve abstractive summarization [18]. This approach goes beyond mere content extraction; it includes content rewriting and is a fusion of two significant Natural Language Processing subtasks [15]: Natural Language Understanding and Natural Language Generation.

Long text summarization typically employs fusion techniques, namely the combined use of extractive and abstractive methods [7,18]. The screenplay summary task has also received wide attention, [8] used TRIPOD dataset to train the GraphTP model to identify turning point (TP) scenes. [6] used a Transformer model to capture long-term contextual information based on GraphTP. In the COLING 2022 shared task part 1, [9] employed a two-stage summarization approach focused on generating plots for given movie scripts. [4] adopted a summarization strategy that combines extractive and abstractive techniques and enhanced the two-stage summarization with script attribute information to achieve the movie script summarization task.

The development of text summarization technology relies heavily on domain-specific datasets. Generative summarization tasks have been applied to datasets in various forms such as TV series (TVRecap, SUMMSCREEN), movies (NARRASUM), and conferences (AMI, ICIS, QMSum) [2]. These datasets primarily consist of conversational text and include a significant amount of colloquial vocabulary. Summarization tasks are crucial for extracting plots and event lines conveyed indirectly in the conversational content.

Currently, addressing long text summarization based on large-scale pre-trained language models (PLM) has led to the mainstream seq2seq framework [12]. In this framework, Encoder-Decoder models are limited in their ability to handle long sequences, resulting in issues such as the contraction of the optimization search space and significant time consumption during long sequence decoding and inference. Furthermore, existing datasets are typically coarse-grained text-summary pairs, lacking fine-grained aligned text for fine-tuning large language models, which limits the use of domain-specific data.

To address the aforementioned challenges, this paper proposes a two-stage screenplay plot summary generation method to tackle the issue of weak long sequence encoding capabilities. It introduces an unsupervised text matching method to create datasets for aligning scene text with plot summaries. Furthermore, parameter perturbation is employed to efficiently fine-tune the Pretrained Language Model.

2   Method

The descriptive framework of our method, as shown in Fig. 1, mainly consists of three parts: preprocessing, extractor, and generator. The T4S, a pipeline synopsis summary generation method, consists of two stages: utilizing the GraphTP extractor to capture the TP scenarios and fine-tuning PLM to generate a summary of the TPs.

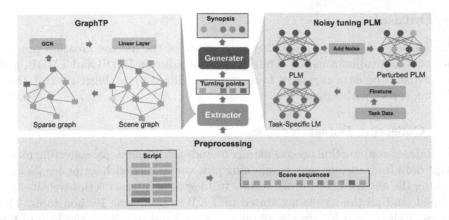

Fig. 1. The framework of T4S.

The preprocessing phase divides the unstructured script into scene text sequences. Specifically, following the analysis in [13], the use of "INT, EXT, INT/EXT" in scriptwriting typically indicates the beginning of a new scene. Naturally, the script's scene sequence can be represented as follows:

$$V = [v_1, \ldots, v_n] = Split(Script). \tag{1}$$

The extractor employs the GraphTP model, which uses a graph structure to represent the content interactions between scene texts, as follows:

$$G = (V, E), \tag{2}$$

$$TPs = [TP_1, TP_2, TP_3, TP_4, TP_5]$$
$$= GraphTP(G), \tag{3}$$

where V represents scenes, and E represents the edges between scene nodes. Additionally, it improves the overall inference speed and computational efficiency by setting a similarity threshold between nodes, eliminating nodes with weak semantic information.

The generator takes the extracted TPs scene and performs extractive compression to form the final plot summary. During the generator's fine-tuning phase, the Noisy tuning method is used, injecting parameter perturbation in the early stages of model fine-tuning. For any PLMs with N parameter matrices $[W_1, W_2, \ldots, W_N]$, the parameter matrices after adding perturbations can be represented as:

$$\left[W_i + U\left(-\frac{\lambda}{2}, \frac{\lambda}{2}\right) * std(W_i), 1 \leq i \leq N\right] \in \tilde{W}. \tag{4}$$

Next, applying the collected dataset to the fine-tuning process of the PLM can be represented as:

$$PLM_{task} = PLM(\tilde{W}, MovieSUM). \tag{5}$$

3   Dataset

This section will provide a detailed description of the dataset creation process and its statistical information. The data is sourced from IMDB and TMDB, and an unsupervised data alignment framework is utilized to establish a text dataset aligning scenes with summaries.

3.1   Collecting Dataet

The dataset construction process mainly includes multiple steps: collecting movie script data from various sources, aligning plot summaries with script scenes, and filtering the aligned text. Firstly, scripts from several internet script websites are scraped, and all the scripts are stored in TXT format using Python tools. The names of all the movies are also obtained. Simultaneously, with the help of the TMDB website, the movie's identifier on IMDB is acquired, and this identifier is used to retrieve the movie's plot summary, creating script-summary pairs. Next, script parsing and coreference resolution methods are used to obtain semantically enriched scene-summary pairs. Finally, text pairs that do not match the character information in the script are filtered out.

3.2   Dataet Statistics

MovieSUM includes 1627 movies with synopsis content, and the distribution of movie genres is shown in Fig. 2. From the results, it is evident that the most common movie genres are Action, Comedy, and Drama, with 459, 321, and 308 movies, respectively. Following that, other prevalent genres include Crime, Biography, Adventure, and Horror, with 132, 120, 100, and 88 movies, respectively. Additionally, the remaining movies are primarily of the Animation genre, with a total of 61.

In the text matching phase, two unsupervised methods were used to generate two subdatasets, and their data statistics are shown in Table 1. Both datasets include text pairs from movie scripts and summaries where the summary sentences are greater than 10. Clearly, the number of text pairs decreased by more than 35% after filtering. The dataset generated using the BM25 [5] matching method includes 1016 movies, 64,599 scene-summary text pairs, with an average summary sentence length of 25.66 and an average scene text length of 1125. The dataset collected using SBERT [11] includes data from 941 movies, comprising 59,017 text pairs, with an average summary sentence length of 25.66 and an average scene text length of 490. From the results, it is evident that the BM25-generated dataset is larger by 76 movies, both datasets have similar average summary sentence lengths, but the average scene length matched by BM25 is significantly higher than that matched by SBERT. This result is due to the differences in the similarity calculation process between the two methods, with BM25 being word-level matching and SBERT being sentence-level matching. Longer texts benefit more from word-level matching, while excessively long texts contain a lot of redundant semantic information, leading to lower matching rates with SBERT.

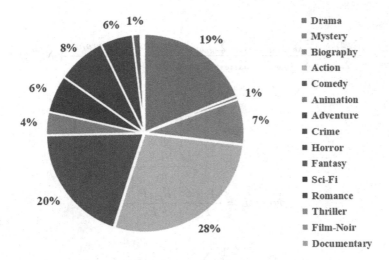

Fig. 2. Movie genre statistics.

Table 1. MovieSUM text pair statistics.

Mathing methods	Count	Scence–summary	Average length of summary	Average length of scene
BM25	1016	64599	25.66	1125
SBERT	941	59017	25.65	490

4 Experiences and Results

4.1 Experimental Setup

The data used in experiments include text pairs matched by the SBERT algorithm (referred to as SBERT), text pairs matched by the BM25 algorithm (referred to as BM25), and the TRIPOD dataset. The first two datasets are used to train the generator in the T4S framework, while the TRIPOD dataset is used to test the generator at the summary level. The perturbation level parameter λ is set to 0.2 during the early stages of model training. The model training process uses the Transformer library, with an initial learning rate set to $2e^{-5}$ and the Adam optimizer. The batch size per GPU is set to 8, and training is performed for 10 epochs. Additionally, early stopping, NoisyTune, and learning rate decay strategies are used. During the prediction phase, beam search is set to 4. All experiments were conducted on servers equipped with two 2080 Ti (12GB) GPUs.

The quality of the generated summaries is evaluated using ROUGE and BERT score. ROUGE scores[1] include ROUGE-1, ROUGE-2, and ROUGE-L, while BERT scoress [17] include Precision, Recall, and F1. These scores are defined as follows:

---

[1] https://pypi.org/project/rouge-score/.

$$rougeN = \frac{\sum_{S\in\{Reference\ Summaries\}}\sum_{gram_n\in S} Count_{match}(gram_n)}{\sum_{S\in\{Reference\ Summaries\}}\sum_{gram_n\in S} Count(gram_n)}, \; N = \{1,2\}, \quad (6)$$

$$R_{lcs} = \frac{LCS(X,Y)}{m_X}, \tag{7}$$

$$P_{lcs} = \frac{LCS(X,Y)}{n_Y}, \tag{8}$$

$$rougeL = \frac{(1+\beta^2)R_{lcs}P_{lcs}}{P_{lcs} + \beta^2 P_{lcs}}, \tag{9}$$

$$P_{bert} = \frac{1}{|\hat{x}|} \sum_{\hat{x}_j \in \hat{x}} \max_{x_i \in x} \mathbf{x}_i^\top \hat{\mathbf{x}}_j, \tag{10}$$

$$R_{bert} = \frac{1}{|x|} \sum_{x_i \in x} \max_{\hat{x}_j \in \hat{x}} \mathbf{x}_i^\top \hat{\mathbf{x}}_j, \tag{11}$$

$$F_{bert} = 2\frac{P_{bert} \cdot R_{bert}}{P_{bert} + R_{bert}}, \tag{12}$$

where, n represents the length of $gram_n$, and $Count_{match}(gram_n)$ is the maximum co-occurrence of n-grams between the generated summary and the reference summary. $Count(gram_n)$ represents the number of n-grams in the reference summary. m_X and n_Y represent the lengths of the reference summary X and the generated summary Y, $LCS(\cdot)$ denotes the longest common subsequence between X and Y, and β is a hyperparameter. $\mathbf{x}_i^\top \hat{\mathbf{x}}_j$ represents the lexical inner product between reference summary $\mathbf{x}$ and generated summary $\hat{\mathbf{x}}$, and $|\cdot|$ is used to normalize the accumulated inner product result.

4.2   Comparing Results

This section compares the summarization performance of T4S with several baseline models on different datasets. The baseline models compared include the following:

1. t5-small [10]: The t5 model treats all text tasks (translation, question answering, classification, etc.) as text-to-text tasks and can handle multiple tasks without changing the model, loss function, and hyperparameters, among others. The model size is 242MB.
2. allenai/led-base-16384 (led-base) [1]: The led (Longformer-Encoder-Decoder) model is designed for long document summarization and question-answering tasks. Led replicates the positional embedding matrix of BART-base 16 times, enabling it to handle longer input texts, up to 16K tokens. The model size is 648MB.

3. philschmid/bart-large-cnn-samsum (bart-large)[2]: This model is based on the BART-large pre-trained model and is fine-tuned on the SAMSum dialogue dataset. The model size is 1.63GB.

4. MingZhong/DialogLED-base-16384 (DialogLM) [19]: An extended model built on top of the led model, specifically trained on a long dialogue dataset. It uses window-based denoising as a pre-training task and is suitable for dialogue understanding and summarization. The model size is 1.858GB.

The results of the text evaluation metrics for the above methods are presented in Table 2. Overall, the smallest model, t5-small, performs the worst across various evaluation metrics. The T4S model outperforms in several metrics and leads significantly. However, the DialogLM model, which is trained on dialogue data like T4S, performs less effectively than the bart-large model. In long document summarization, T4S benefits from the NoisyTune fine-tuning strategy, while in short document summarization, T4S shows overall better performance. This is mainly due to the difference resulting from increasing the input text length while keeping the reference summary length the same. In summary, differences in training data, model sizes, and variations in fine-tuning strategies all influence the model's performance.

5   Ablation Experiments

This section presents experiments conducted on data generated by different matching algorithms to compare the impact of these algorithms on text generation models. The experimental results are shown in Table 3. In terms of evaluation metrics, models trained on SBERT-generated data perform better overall, with the exception of the rouge2 metric, where models trained on BM25 data perform slightly better. In terms of training time, BM25 requires more time compared to SBERT, mainly due to the larger volume and length of the BM25 data. On the same dataset, the models benefit from extensive pre-training of larger models and retaining substantial prior knowledge, leading to roughly a 2x improvement in rouge scores. SBERT outperforms BM25 by 1.09% and 0.83% in rouge1 and rougeL, respectively. In terms of Bert scores, SBERT outperforms BM25 by 0.42%, 0.29%, and 0.35%. These results are due to the fact that the input text for SBERT is much smaller compared to BM25's input text, and the generation model can only handle inputs up to a length of 256 tokens. The t5-small model does not perform well under the same epoch, mainly because smaller models require more epochs to optimize their performance.

---

[2] https://huggingface.co/philschmid/bart-large-cnn-samsum.

Table 2. Performance comparison.The bolded font is the optimal value of the corresponding dataset. N denotes NoisyTune.

Dataset	Model	rouge1	rouge2	rougeL	P_{bert}	R_{bert}	F_{bert}
BM25	t5-small	0.101	0.008	0.088	0.823	0.825	0.824
	led-base	0.089	0.007	0.078	0.813	0.822	0.817
	bart-large	0.146	0.016	0.110	0.823	0.835	0.828
	DialogLM	0.104	0.010	0.076	0.788	0.827	0.807
	T4S	0.190	0.048	0.167	0.856	0.844	0.850
	T4S_N	**0.194**	**0.053**	**0.171**	**0.861**	**0.849**	**0.855**
SBERT	t5-small	0.105	0.007	0.092	0.826	0.827	0.826
	led-base	0.099	0.007	0.086	0.816	0.824	0.820
	bart-large	0.146	0.015	0.111	0.826	0.8365	0.830
	DialogLM	0.119	0.009	0.087	0.794	0.827	0.811
	T4S	**0.205**	0.048	**0.179**	**0.865**	**0.852**	**0.858**
	T4S_N	0.203	**0.050**	0.177	0.864	0.851	0.857
TRIPOD	t5-small	0.073	0.004	0.063	0.807	0.813	0.810
	led-base	0.097	0.003	0.080	0.811	0.813	0.812
	bart-large	0.163	0.013	0.112	0.827	0.833	0.830
	DialogLM	0.101	0.006	0.071	0.776	0.816	0.796
	T4S	0.150	0.011	0.125	0.844	**0.828**	0.834
	T4S_N	**0.168**	**0.019**	**0.129**	**0.852**	0.825	**0.835**

Table 3. Training generated model with different data.

Metrics	BM25		SBERT	
	t5-small	led	t5-small	led
rouge1	0.1061	0.1939	0.1161	**0.2048**
rouge2	0.0104	**0.0528**	0.0109	0.0486
rougeL	0.0984	0.1707	0.1065	**0.179**
P_{bert}	0.8373	0.8605	0.8428	**0.8647**
R_{bert}	0.8301	0.8493	0.8326	**0.8522**
F_{bert}	0.8333	0.8546	0.8374	**0.8581**
Training time	2.32H	28.9H	2.07H	26.05H

Additionally, this section compares the impact of NoisyTune on the T4S model using text pairs matched with BM25, as shown in Fig. 3. Figure 3a shows that NoisyTune outperforms Finetuning in terms of rouge scores, but it's worth noting that at epoch 2, the rouge1 and rougeL scores for finetuning are similar to the corresponding scores for NoisyTune. Figure 3b shows that NoisyTune exhibits more significant loss reduction. The advantage of loss reduction gradually increases after the first epoch, resulting in a maximum loss difference of 0.2488 between the two fine-tuning methods. The results indicate that perturbations on the input side are beneficial for training large-scale language models, leading to a significant improvement in text generation evaluation metrics.

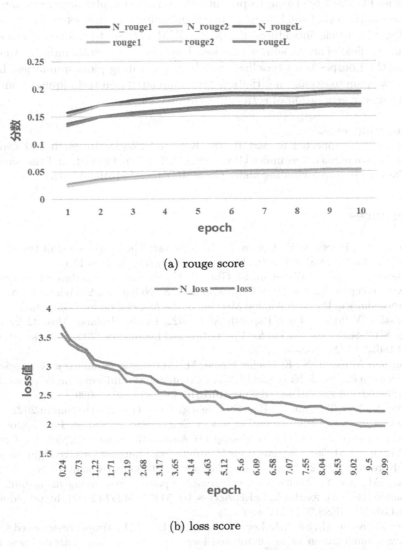

(a) rouge score

(b) loss score

Fig. 3. Comparison of led finetuning Results, N represents NoisyTune.

6   Conclusion

In this paper, we introduces a method for generating plot summaries of movie scripts, referred to as T4S. It employs a two-stage strategy to accomplish domain-specific long-form summarization. This approach involves the extraction of key scenes and content rewriting to produce the final script plot summary, addressing the limitations of weak long sequence encoding capabilities in PLMs. Additionally, the article introduces the MovieSUM dataset to address the lack of data in the field of script summarization. Experimental results indicate that the T4S method outperforms baseline models in generating plot summaries. In the future, we plan to explore multi-stage text summarization techniques to enhance the automatic generation of script plot summaries.

Acknowledgments.
This work was supported in part by the Key Technologies Research and Development Program of Shenzhen under Grant JSGG20210802154400001, and the Shenzhen Foundational Research Funding under Grant JCYJ20220818102415032.

References

1. Beltagy, I., Peters, M.E., Cohan, A.: Longformer: The long-document transformer. CoRR abs/2004.05150 (2020), https://arxiv.org/abs/2004.05150
2. Chen, M., Chu, Z., Wiseman, S., Gimpel, K.: Summscreen: a dataset for abstractive screenplay summarization. In: Muresan, S., Nakov, P., Villavicencio, A. (eds.) Proceedings of the 60th Annual Meeting of the Association for Computational Linguistics (Volume 1: Long Papers), ACL 2022, Dublin, Ireland, May 22–27, 2022, pp. 8602–8615. Association for Computational Linguistics (2022). https://doi.org/10.18653/v1/2022.acl-long.589
3. Ibrahim Altmami, N., El Bachir Menai, M.: Automatic summarization of scientific articles: a survey. J. King Saud Univ. - Computer and Information Sciences 34(4), 1011–1028 (2022). https://doi.org/10.1016/j.jksuci.2020.04.020
4. Kim, E., Yoo, T., Cho, G., Bae, S., Cheong, Y.G.: The CreativeSumm 2022 shared task: a two-stage summarization model using scene attributes. In: Mckeown, K. (ed.) Proceedings of The Workshop on Automatic Summarization for Creative Writing, pp. 51–56. Association for Computational Linguistics, Gyeongju, Republic of Korea (Oct 2022). https://aclanthology.org/2022.creativesumm-1.8
5. Kim, M., Ko, Y.: Multitask fine-tuning for passage re-ranking using bm25 and pseudo relevance feedback. IEEE Access 10, 54254–54262 (2022). https://doi.org/10.1109/ACCESS.2022.3176894
6. Lee, M., Kwon, H., Shin, J., Lee, W., Jung, B., Lee, J.H.: Transformer-based screenplay summarization using augmented learning representation with dialogue information. In: Akoury, N., Brahman, F., Chaturvedi, S., Clark, E., Iyyer, M., Martin, L.J. (eds.) Proceedings of the Third Workshop on Narrative Understanding, pp. 56–61. Association for Computational Linguistics, Virtual (Jun 2021). https://doi.org/10.18653/v1/2021.nuse-1.6
7. Ma, T., Pan, Q., Rong, H., Qian, Y., Tian, Y., Al-Nabhan, N.: T-bertsum: topic-aware text summarization based on bert. IEEE Trans. Comput. Social Syst. 9(3), 879–890 (JUN 2022). https://doi.org/10.1109/TCSS.2021.3088506

8. Papalampidi, P., Keller, F., Lapata, M.: Movie summarization via sparse graph construction. In: Thirty-Fifth AAAI Conference on Artificial Intelligence, AAAI 2021, Thirty-Third Conference on Innovative Applications of Artificial Intelligence, IAAI 2021, The Eleventh Symposium on Educational Advances in Artificial Intelligence, EAAI 2021, Virtual Event, February 2–9, 2021, pp. 13631–13639. AAAI Press (2021). https://doi.org/10.1609/AAAI.V35I15.17607

9. Pu, D., Hong, X., Lin, P.J., Chang, E., Demberg, V.: Two-stage movie script summarization: an efficient method for low-resource long document summarization. In: Mckeown, K. (ed.) Proceedings of The Workshop on Automatic Summarization for Creative Writing, pp. 57–66. Association for Computational Linguistics, Gyeongju, Republic of Korea (Oct 2022). https://aclanthology.org/2022.creativesumm-1.9

10. Raffel, C., et al.: Exploring the limits of transfer learning with a unified text-to-text transformer. J. Mach. Learn. Res. **21**(140), 1–67 (2020), http://jmlr.org/papers/v21/20-074.html

11. Reimers, N., Gurevych, I.: Sentence-bert: sentence embeddings using siamese bert-networks. In: Proceedings of the 2019 Conference on Empirical Methods in Natural Language Processing. Association for Computational Linguistics (11 2019). https://arxiv.org/abs/1908.10084

12. Upadhyay, A., Bhavsar, N., Bhatnagar, A., Singh, M., Motlicek, P.: Automatic summarization for creative writing: BART based pipeline method for generating summary of movie scripts. In: Mckeown, K. (ed.) Proceedings of The Workshop on Automatic Summarization for Creative Writing, pp. 44–50. Association for Computational Linguistics, Gyeongju, Republic of Korea (Oct 2022), https://aclanthology.org/2022.creativesumm-1.7

13. Wang, D., Cheng, L., Liu, H., Li, R., Wang, H., Liu, H.: Script2graph: auto-construct screenplay text world by mining contextual information. In: 2023 IEEE 3rd International Conference on Software Engineering and Artificial Intelligence (SEAI), pp. 288–293 (2023). https://doi.org/10.1109/SEAI59139.2023.10217409

14. Yadav, D., Katna, R., Yadav, A.K., Morato, J.: Feature based automatic text summarization methods: a comprehensive state-of-the-art survey. IEEE Access **10**, 133981–134003 (2022)

15. Zhang, D., Li, W.: An Improved Math Word Problem (MWP) Model Using Unified Pretrained Language Model (UniLM) for Pretraining. Computational Intelligence and Neuroscience 2022 (Jul 2022). https://doi.org/10.1155/2022/7468286, publisher: Hindawi

16. Zhang, M., Zhou, G., Yu, W., Huang, N., Liu, W.: A comprehensive survey of abstractive text summarization based on deep learning. Comput. Intell. Neurosci. **2022** (AUG 1 2022). https://doi.org/10.1155/2022/7132226

17. Zhang, T., Kishore, V., Wu, F., Weinberger, K.Q., Artzi, Y.: Bertscore: evaluating text generation with BERT. In: 8th International Conference on Learning Representations, ICLR 2020, Addis Ababa, Ethiopia, April 26–30 (2020). OpenReview.net (2020). https://openreview.net/forum?id=SkeHuCVFDr

18. Zhang, Y., et al.: Summ^n: A multi-stage summarization framework for long input dialogues and ocuments. In: proceedings of the 60th Annual Meeting of the Association for Computational Linguistics (ACL 2022), VOL 1: (LONG PAPERS), pp. 1592–1604. Assoc Computat Linguist; Amazon Sci; loomberg Engn; Google Res; Liveperson; Meta; Baidu; ByteDance; DeepMind; Grammarly; GTCOM; IBM; Megagon Labs; Microsoft; Alibaba Grp; Bosch; Cohere; G Res; ServiceNow; Relativity; Naver; ASAPP; Duolingo; BabelSpace; Spotiry; Adobe; D & I Special Initiat; AppTek; YaiGlobal; Aixplain; Apple (2022), 60th Annual Meeting of the Association-for-Computational-Linguistics (ACL), Dublin, IRELAND, MAY 22-27, 2022

19. Zhong, M., Liu, Y., Xu, Y., Zhu, C., Zeng, M.: Dialoglm: pre-trained model for long dialogue understanding and summarization. In: Thirty-Sixth AAAI Conference on Artificial Intelligence, AAAI 2022, Thirty-Fourth Conference on Innovative Applications of Artificial Intelligence, IAAI 2022, The Twelveth Symposium on Educational Advances in Artificial Intelligence, EAAI 2022 Virtual Event, February 22 - March 1, 2022. pp. 11765–11773. AAAI Press (2022). https://doi.org/10.1609/AAAI.V36I10.21432

Application Track

Multi-Factor Water Level Prediction Based on IndRNN-Attention

Haifeng Lv[1], Yishuang Ning[2(✉)], Ke Ning[2], Sheng He[2], and Hongquan Lin[1]

[1] Guangxi Key Laboratory of Machine Vision and Intelligent Control, WuZhou University, Wuzhou, China

[2] Kingdee International Software Group Company Limited, Kingdee Research, Shenzhen, China
ningyishuang@126.com

Abstract. Accurate prediction of hydrologic time series, such as water level and water volume, is essential for effective water resource management and plays a crucial role in detecting water transfers. Existing water level prediction methods usually only consider a single factor (such as the historical water level data), and do not fully consider other factors such as flows from the upstream stations that affect the water level. To address this problem, in this paper, we propose a multi-factor water level prediction model that combines an independently recurrent neural network (IndRNN) with an attention mechanism. Our model overcomes the gradient disappearance problem of traditional RNNs and improves prediction accuracy by encoding the historical input data that influence the water level. Additionally, by combining with the attention mechanism, the model is capable of capturing the contributions of specific historical moments for water level prediction. Experimental results demonstrate the effectiveness of our proposed method. Besides, the findings of this paper have practical implications for industry supervisors and cargo-carrying ships, providing scientific guidance for precise ship pre-scheduling.

Keyword: Time series · Water level prediction · IndRNN · Attention

1 Introduction

Water level prediction refers to the prediction of the future water level at a particular location, based on historical data and relevant environmental factors such as rainfall, tides, and outbound flow from upstream stations. Currently, to predict the water level accurately is very essential for the comprehensive utilization of water resources. It plays an important role in effective water resource management, flood prevention, and environmental protection. Accurate and timely prediction of water level is crucial for ensuring the safety of communities residing near rivers and optimizing water resource allocation.

When it comes to the water level prediction task, existing methods mainly use the single factor for prediction. For example, In 2013, [1] proposed to predict the water level of the Klang River based on the historical water level data by using the autoregressive integrated moving average model (ARIMA) and adaptive neuro-fuzzy inference system (ANFIS). In 2019, [2] studied the prediction of water level in the Yangtze River using an improved single factor-based least squares support vector machine (LSSVM) model. In recent years, deep learning based methods have been arising and achieved significant results in various fields. Researchers have tried to utilize this kind of methods for water level prediction. For instance, [3] constructed a single-site water level prediction model based on the long and short-term memory (LSTM) model for the Jialing River. However, due to the complex nature of river systems and the influence of various factors (such as the historical water level data and the flows from the upstream stations), achieving accurate water level prediction remains a challenging task.

To address this problem, this paper proposes a multi-factor water level prediction method. In this paper, the historical water level data and the flows from the upstream stations are viewed as the two kinds of factors. To integrate these factors, we utilize the IndRNN based method, which can be designed as multiple input channels, where each channel represents a different factor. In this case, one channel represents the historical water level data, while the other channel represents the historical flow data. Each channel has its own set of weights and connections within the IndRNN architecture. Besides, to capture the long-term dependencies of each factor, we combine the IndRNN with attention mechanism to make the model focus on the most relevant parts of the input sequence for better prediction. Extensive of experiments conducted on the Xijiang River data demonstrate the effectiveness of our proposed method.

The contributions of this paper are as follows:

1. We propose a multi-factor water level prediction model based on the IndRNN-Attention architecture.
2. Extensive of experiments conducted on the Xijiang River data demonstrate the effectiveness of the proposed multi-factor water level prediction model.

The findings of this research will contribute to the advancement of water level prediction methodologies, offering insights into the application of deep learning techniques in hydrological modeling. Furthermore, the results will provide valuable guidance for decision-makers, hydrologists, and water resource managers involved in flood control, water allocation, and environmental management along the Xijiang River.

2 Related Work

Past research on water level prediction has mainly focused on utilizing traditional machine learning methods, such as ARIMA and support vector regression (SVR). For example, [3] used the traditional ARIMA model to transform non-stationary time series data into stationary time series ones, and then establish a regression model with the dependent variable against its error stochastic term and lag value. [4] proposed an improved ARIMA model to predict the monthly water flow of the heroin reservoir in New Mexico, USA, and achieved a significant improvement over the index person coefficient. [5] analyzed the historical water level time series data of Hankou, Jianli, and Anqing, achieving a high fitting effect of daily average water level by using the ARIMA model. However, due to the inherent feature of the ARIMA model that cannot model long time historical data, it still has limited capability for improving the prediction effectiveness.

Recent trends of water level prediction are to utilize deep learning based methods that are capable to capture short and long time context information for modeling. For instance,

[6] used the AR-RNN model to predict the water level of Qingxi River, achieving a low relative error. [7] constructed a single-site water level prediction model based on the long and short-term memory (LSTM) model for the Jialing River. [8] proposed an attention-based LSTM model for river flow forecasting. However, these methods only use single factor such as the historical water level information, ignoring the influence of other factors such as flows from the upstream stations.

3   Approaches

3.1   Motivation

Water level prediction is a complex task that is influenced by multiple factors, such as historical water level data of the site, and flows from the upstream stations. Therefore, a model that can consider both the two kinds of factors is important for water level prediction. To integrate the two kinds of factors, we propose to use the IndRNN based method that has been widely adopted for modeling multiple factors or features in many tasks [9–11]. Moreover, given the inherent time-series characteristics of water level data, IndRNN [12] is capable of capturing the long-term dependencies of the sequential data. Besides, by integrating with the attention mechanism, the model can focus on the most relevant parts of the input sequence for better prediction.

3.2   Architecture of the Proposed Method

Figure 1 shows the overall architecture of our proposed method. As can be seen from this figure, it consists of four layers: the input layer, the encoder layer, the attention layer and the output layer.

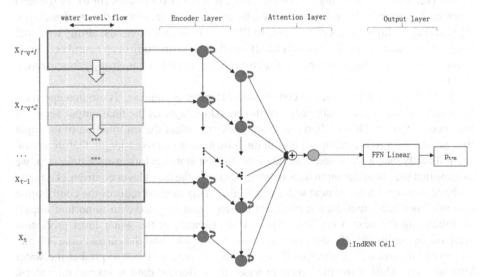

Fig. 1. The overall architecture of our proposed method.

Firstly, in the input layer, given an input sequence $(x_{t-q}, x_{t-q+1}, ..., x_{t-1})$ with q time steps prior to the current time node t, the i-th input includes multiple factors which are the historical water level data and the corresponding flow values from the upstream tributaries. Both the two kinds of factors are given as the input to the encoder layer which uses IndRNN to output an H-dimensional feature vector representation by iterating the following equation from $t = 1$ to T:

$$h_t = \sigma(Wx_t + U \odot h_{t-1} + b), \tag{1}$$

where h_t is the hidden state at time step t, x_t is the input at time step t, W is the weight matrix, b is the bias term, U is a diagonal matrix with the diagonal elements being the max singular values of W, and σ is the activation function such as ReLU or sigmoid. The operation $U \odot h_{t-1}$ denotes an element-wise multiplication between the diagonal matrix U and the hidden state h_{t-1}. In IndRNN, the neurons in each layer are independent of each other, and their connections are achieved by stacking multiple layers of IndRNN. The hidden state of the n-th neuron at time step t can be calculated by the following formulation:

$$h_{n,t} = \sigma(W_n x_t + U_n \odot h_{n,t-1} + b_n), \tag{2}$$

where $h_{n,t}$ is the hidden state of the n-th neuron at time step t, x_t is the input at time step t, W_n is the weight matrix of the n-th neuron, U_n is the recurrent weight matrix of the n-th neuron, $\odot$ denotes element-wise multiplication, and b_n is the bias term of the n-th neuron. Σ is the activation function such as ReLU or sigmoid.

In IndRNN, each neuron only takes the output of the previous time step's hidden state and the input of the current time step, and each neuron independently processes a type of spatiotemporal pattern. Traditional RNNs are generally regarded as multilayer perceptrons with time-shared parameters, while IndRNN presents a new perspective of independently aggregating spatial patterns (in w) over time steps (in u). In the next layer, each neuron independently receives the output of all neurons in the previous layer. By stacking multiple layers of neurons, IndRNN not only improves the ability to model long-time sequences but also reduces the difficulty of constructing deep neural networks. In addition, using activation functions such as ReLU, IndRNN has strong generalization ability.

Secondly, in order to obtain a contextual vector representation, a common approach is to treat the last hidden state vector of the encoding layer as the final output vector of the encoding layer. This method can to some extent reflect the information of the input time series, but it is difficult to encode all the information in a fixed-length feature vector. If we directly take a weighted average of the hidden state vectors at each time step, we assume that the historical input data at any time step in the input layer contributes equally to the representation of the next water level value. This method reduces the contribution of some historical input data at certain time steps that may have an important impact on predicting the next water level value. For example, in the water level prediction scenario, assuming that the time unit is measured in hours, and the current time is 4 pm, the historical data of the previous 30 time steps is taken as input to predict the water level at 4 pm. During the prediction process, the historical data at several time steps, such as 3 pm and 4 pm yesterday and 2 pm and 3 pm today, are most important for accurate prediction, and their weights should be the highest. Therefore, we use a time-level attention mechanism to obtain the time-step information that has an important impact on predicting the water level.

Given a time series $s = (c_1, c_2, ..., c_L)$ of water level and flow data with length L, let $h_{jt} \in \mathbb{R}^{d_h}$ be the vector representation of the water level and flow input data at time j in sequence s at time t, which is computed by the encoding layer. The calculation of the time-level attention consists of the following three processes:

1) Compute attention weights. First, h_{jt} is fed into a feed-forward neural network to obtain its attention weight vector a, where the j-th element of a represents the weight at the j-th time step. Specifically, the calculation of a is given by:

$$a_j = soft\max(W_a^T * \tanh(W_a * h_{jt} + b_a)), \tag{3}$$

where W_a and b_a are learnable parameters, W_a is the weight matrix, softmax is the normalization function, and tanh is the activation function.

2) Compute weighted vector. The attention weight a is multiplied by the feature vector h output by the encoding layer to obtain the weighted vector c. Specifically, the calculation of c is given by:

$$c = \sum a_j * h_j, \tag{4}$$

where h_j represents the feature vector output by the encoding layer.

3) Update feature vector. The weighted vector c and the feature vector h output by the encoding layer are concatenated and fed into a feed-forward neural network to obtain the final feature vector h_{new}. Specifically, the calculation of h_{new} is given by:

$$h_{new} = \sigma(W_h * [h, c] + b_h), \tag{5}$$

where W_h and b_h are learnable parameters, $[h, c]$ represents the concatenated vector of h and c, and σ is the activation function such as ReLU or sigmoid.

Finally, after obtaining the final vector representation h_{new} from the attention layer, it is fed into a fully connected layer to compute the confidence score of predicting the water level value at the future m-th time step. Specifically, the calculation of the confidence score is given by:

$$o = f(W_o * h_{new} + b_o), \tag{6}$$

where $\mathbf{w}_o \in \mathbb{R}^{k \times d_h}$ and $\mathbf{b}_o \in \mathbb{R}^k$ are the weight matrix and bias term of the fully connected layer, respectively. Since the output is a single factor, which is the predicted water level value, k is equal to 1 in this case. f is the activation function, such as softmax or sigmoid, which maps the output of the fully connected layer to a probability distribution over the possible values of the future water level at the m-th time step.

The mean squared error (MSE) loss function is chosen as the objective function. Given a training set $T = \{(s^i, y^i)\}$, the MSE loss is defined as:

$$J(\Theta) = \frac{1}{N} \cdot \sum_{i=1}^{|N|} (y^i - o^i(\Theta))^2, \tag{7}$$

where N is the number of training samples, y^i is the true water level value at the i-th time step, o^i is the predicted water level value at the i-th time step, and the sum is over all N training samples. The MSE loss measures the average squared difference between the true water level values and the predicted water level values, and is a commonly used loss function for regression problems. The goal of the training process is to minimize the MSE loss on the training set, which is achieved by adjusting the network parameters through backpropagation and gradient descent. Θ represents all the parameters used in the model, including the weights and biases of the encoding layer, the time-level attention layer, the fully connected layer, and any other layers or components that may be present in the model. These parameters are learned during the training process by minimizing the MSE loss on the training set through gradient descent and backpropagation.

The IndRNN-Attention model can accept multiple factors (including the flow of multiple upstream stations and the water level of the station to be predicted) as inputs and output a single factor prediction result for the water level.

3.3 Details of Model Training Scheme

In the model architecture, we basically followed the deep neural network framework, which uses the IndRNN-Attention architecture implemented with Keras 2.3.1 and Tensorflow 1.15.0. To optimize the performance of our proposed IndRNN-Attention model, we conducted a systematic exploration of various parameter settings, including the number of epochs, layers, learning rate, hidden size, loss function, and more. To prevent the model from overfitting, we also used a gradient clipping technique where the dropout rate was set to 0.3. Detailed settings are presented in Table 1.

Table 1. Detailed model parameter settings

Parameter name	value
number of layers	2
hidden size	24
epochs	60
optimizer	SGD
batch size	64
activation	ReLU
loss	MSE
learning rate	0.04
dropout rate	0.3

4 Experiments

4.1 Experimental Setup

Dataset. To evaluate the effectiveness of our proposed method, we use flow and water level data from stations located in the Xijiang River Basin, including Wuzhou (WZ), Changzhou (CZ), Jingnan (JN), Datengxia (DTX), and Guiping (GP) from 2020 to 2021. The relevant information for these stations is shown in Table 2, including station ID, station name, time required for the station's flow to reach the Wuzhou station, data type (flow/water level), and data weight (the greater the weight, the greater the impact of the factor on the model). Data were collected every hour, with a total of 12,984 records. The original data are shown in Table 3, where the data type for the Wuzhou station is water level, unit: m, and for other stations is flow, unit: m^3/s. Five-fold cross-validation is used, in which the training data are randomly divided into five sets, with one set used as the testing set and the remaining four sets used as the training set.

Table 2. The relevant information for Xijiang stations

id	name	cost (/h)	type	weight
829760	Datengxia	9	flow	1.0
109760	Guiping	8	flow	0.95
10000017	Jingnan	10	flow	1.0
159765	Changzhou	2	flow	0.9
10000003	Wuzhou	0	water level	1.0

Preprocessing. To eliminate the impact of sensor anomalies and missing data, the interpolation technique was used to process these data in this paper. Specifically, for missing or anomalous values, the mean of the data from the most recent n time points $(x_1, x_2, ..., x_n)$ was used to fill the gaps. After processing the data, it was observed that the sizes of the data were not consistent due to the different units of the factors, such as flow in cubic meters per second (m^3/s) and water level in meters (m). This inconsistency could affect the effectiveness of the model. Therefore, all factor values were normalized during the data processing stage. This approach could help the model to better identify the relationships between different factors, improve the training convergence speed, and reduce the training time. The expression for the normalized data is as follows:

$$x^* = \frac{x - \min}{\max - \min},\tag{8}$$

where x^* represents the normalized value of the sample data; x represents the original value of the sample data; max and min represent the maximum and minimum values of the sample data for the same feature. After normalization, the range of each feature data for each sample is between 0 and 1.

Table 3. Flow and water level data of multiple stations from 2020 to 2021

date	WZ(m)	CZ(m^3/s)	JN(m^3/s)	DTX(m^3/s)	GP(m^3/s)
2020/7/9 0:00	7.82	6935.1	728	7210	1518.9
2020/7/9 1:00	7.84	6927.3	576	7200	1515.4
2020/7/9 2:00	7.81	6959.2	520	7170	1523.7
2020/7/9 3:00	7.81	6943.1	492	7074	1521.0
2020/7/9 4:00	7.8	6937.6	464	6978	1518.4
2020/7/9 5:00	7.79	6958.2	429	6882	1522.2
2020/7/9 6:00	7.78	6922.1	408	6786	1520.4
2020/7/9 7:00	7.76	6635.4	394	6690	1529.7
...	...	...	...	...	...
2021/12/31 12:00	3.01	2005.7	109	1020	412.4
2021/12/31 13:00	2.92	1697.4	109	1160	409.4
2021/12/31 14:00	2.85	2031.2	109	1100	408.8

Comparison Methods. We compared the performance of the proposed method with some existing methods such as ARIMA, LSTM.and IndRNN only.

Evaluation Metrics. In all the experiments, we evaluate the performance in terms of RMSE, R^2 and NSE [13].

4.2 Experimental Results

4.2.1 Comparison of Predicted Value and Actual Value

To verify the predictive performance of the model, out-of-sample prediction is conducted on the hourly water level data for December 1, 2021, with the unit being meters (m). As shown in Table 4, the predicted values have a smaller error compared to the actual values, with an average relative error of 2.15%, a maximum relative error of only 4.43%, and a maximum absolute error of only 0.12m. The prediction results of this model is capable of providing accurate pre-scheduling vessel information for the Xijiang lock operation scheduling center and provide effective guidance and suggestions for industry regulators and cargo-laden vessels.

4.2.2 Comparison with Other Methods: Case of Wuzhou Station

Table 5 shows the comparison results with other machine learning and deep learning methods. From this table, we can draw the following conclusions: 1) Using LSTM only can achieve good performance (in terms of the three evaluation metrics) compared with other traditional machine learning methods such as ARIMA, indicating that the contextual dependencies are very important for the water level prediction task. 2) To compare with LSTM, IndRNN can better leverage the contextual dependencies for modeling.

Table 4. 12-h water level forecast on December 1, 2021 (unit:m).

Date	actual	predict	relative error	absolute error
2021/12/1 0:00	3.05	3.07	0.0066	0.020
2021/12/1 1:00	3.01	3.05	0.0133	0.040
2021/12/1 2:00	2.98	2.94	0.0134	0.040
2021/12/1 3:00	2.92	2.88	0.0137	0.040
2021/12/1 4:00	2.86	2.80	0.0210	0.060
2021/12/1 5:00	2.83	2.76	0.0247	0.070
2021/12/1 6:00	2.81	2.74	0.0249	0.070
2021/12/1 7:00	2.79	2.73	0.0215	0.060
2021/12/1 8:00	2.78	2.72	0.0216	0.060
2021/12/1 9:00	2.74	2.71	0.0109	0.030
2021/12/1 10:00	2.71	2.59	0.0443	0.120
2021/12/1 11:00	2.68	2.57	0.0410	0.110

3) When multiple factors are used, the performance has been significantly improved.
4) When the attention mechanism is combined with Multi-IndRNN, the performance has improved significantly (2.5% and 2.8% in terms of NSE and R^2, respectively). The reason might be that the incorporation of attention mechanism enables the model to enhance its focus on critical feature components.

Table 5. Comparison results of using different methods. (Single-LSTM: use LSTM and single factor for modeling; Single-IndRNN: use IndRNN and single factor for modeling; Multi-IndRNN: use IndRNN and multiple factors for modeling; Multi-IndRNN-Attention: use IndRNN-Attention and multiple factors for modeling.)

Metrics	ARIMA	Single-LSTM	Single-IndRNN	Multi-IndRNN	Multi-IndRNN-Attention
NSE	0.773	0.818	0.821	0.887	**0.912**
R^2	0.778	0.823	0.827	0.896	**0.924**
RMSE	0.196	0.161	0.158	0.121	**0.103**

4.2.3 Ablation Study

To evaluate the contribution of different factors (the historical water level and flows from the upstream stations), we conduct an ablation study. Experimental results are illustrated in Table 6. As can be seen from this table, the performance of using water level only is slightly higher than using flow in terms of NSR, indicating that water level may be more crucial than flow. Besides, when we use the combination of the historical water level and flow from the upstream station for prediction, it achieves much higher performance than use water level only. These results validate the necessity and effectiveness of taking the historical water level and flow from the upstream station for consideration.

Table 6. Performance of IndRNN-Attention model with different factors on the test set

Model	Multi-factor inputs	NSE	R2	RMSE
Model 1	With the historical water level only	0.893	0.916	0.122
Model 2	With flows from the upstream stations only	0.875	0.891	0.137
Model 3	With both of the two factors	**0.912**	**0.924**	**0.103**

5 Conclusion

In this paper, we propose a novel multi-factor water level prediction method which uses multiple factors including the historical water level data and flows from the upstream stations. To better capture the contextual dependencies and corrections between the two kinds of factors, the IndRNN-Attention model is used where different factors can be designed as different input channels, and each channel has its own set of weights and connections within the IndRNN-Attention architecture. Extensive of experimental results demonstrate the effectiveness of the proposed method and show superior performance over LSTM method and using a single factor. In future, we will mine more relative factors to further improve the performance of water level prediction.

Acknowledgements. This article is supported in part by a grant from Guangxi Key Laboratory of Machine Vision and Intelligent Control, Wuzhou Science and Technology Plan Project(2022A01036), Wuzhou University Education and Teaching Reform Project (Wyjg2022B005, Wyjg2022A035).

References

Galavi, H., Mirzaei, M., Shul, L.T., et al.: Klang River–level forecasting using ARIMA and ANFIS models. J. Am. Water Works Ass. **105**(9), 496–506 (2013)

Guo, T., He, W., Jiang, Z., et al.: An improved LSSVM model for intelligent prediction of the daily water level. Energies **12**(1), 112 (2018)

Ci, B.C., Zhang, P.Y.: Financial time series forecasting based on ARIMALSTM model. Stat. Decis. **38**(11), 145–149 (2022)

Sabzi, H.Z., King, J.P., Abudu, S.: Developing an intelligent expert system for streamflow prediction, integrated in a dynamic decision support system for managing multiple reservoirs: a case study. Expert Syst. Appl. **83**, 145–163 (2017)

Yu, Z.: Research on channel water level prediction based on time series analysis. China Water Transport (Month) **18**(10), 148–150 (2018)

Deo, R.C., Kisi, O., Singh, V.P.: Drought forecasting in eastern Australia using multivariate adaptive regression spline, least square support vector machine and M5Tree model. Atmos. Res. **184**, 149–175 (2017)

Feng, R.: Research on runoff sequence prediction of Jiulong river basin based on LSTM model, Xi'an: Chang'an University (2019)

Noor, F., Haq, S., Rakib, M., et al.: Water level forecasting using spatiotemporal attention-based long short-term memory network. Water **14**(4), 612 (2022)

Lu, S., Zhu, Y., Liu, S., et al.: A tool wear prediction model based on attention mechanism and IndRNN. In: 2022 International Joint Conference on Neural Networks (IJCNN), pp. 1–7. IEEE (2022)

Wu, B., Wang, L., Lv, S.X., et al.: Forecasting oil consumption with attention-based IndRNN optimized by adaptive differential evolution. Appl. Intell. **53**(5), 5473–5496 (2023)

Li, J., Huang, Z., Wang, J.: GDP prediction based on independent recurrent neural network method. Stat. Decis. **36**(14), 24–28 (2020)

Li, S., Li, W., Cook, C., et al.: Independently recurrent neural network (IndRNN): building a longer and deeper RNN, Proceedings of the IEEE Conference on Computer Vision and Pattern Recognition, pp. 5457–5466 (2018)

Krause, P., Boyle, D.P., Bäse, F.: Comparison of different efficiency criteria for hydrological model assessment. Adv. Geosci. **5**, 89–97 (2005)

Ethereum Public Opinion Analysis Based on Attention Mechanism

Xianghan Zheng⑩, Wenyan Zhang⑩, Jianxian Zhang⑩, and Weipeng Xie⁽✉⁾ ⑩

Fuzhou University, Fuzhou, Fujian, China
{xianghan.zheng,211020066}@fzu.edu.cn, 1450628865@qq.com

Abstract. With the rapid development of Ethereum, vast amounts of data are recorded on the blockchain through transactions, encompassing diverse and extensive textual information. While Long Short-Term Memory (LSTM) models have shown remarkable effectiveness in sentiment analysis tasks in recent years, they often encounter situations where different features have equal importance when processing such textual data. Therefore, this study introduces a Bidirectional LSTM model with a Multi-Head Attention mechanism (MABLSTM) designed for sentiment analysis tasks in Ethereum transaction texts. BLSTM consists of two distinct and independent LSTMs that consider information flow from two directions, capturing contextual information from both the past and the future. The outputs from the BLSTM layer are enhanced using a multi-head attention mechanism to amplify the importance of sentiment words and blockchain-specific terms. This paper evaluates the effectiveness of MABLSTM on Ethereum transaction data through experiments conducted on an Ethereum transaction dataset, comparing MABLSTM with CNN, SVM, ABLSTM and ABCDM. The results demonstrate the effectiveness and superiority of MABLSTM in sentiment analysis tasks. This approach accurately analyzes sentiment polarity in Ethereum transaction texts, providing valuable information for Ethereum participants and researchers to support decision-making and emotional analysis.

Keywords: Sentiment Analysis · Ethereum · Deep Learning · Attention Mechanism · BLSTM · MABLST

1 Introduction

With the rapid development of blockchain technology, Ethereum has emerged as the most widely used public smart contract blockchain platform, providing a rich development and execution environment for various applications [1–3]. Meanwhile, Ethereum transactions contain a substantial amount of textual information, expressing users' attitudes and opinions on current social sentiments, which significantly impact market fluctuations and developments. Therefore, accurate classification and analysis of the sentiment within Ethereum transactions can offer valuable market sentiment and emotional insights for participants and researchers, enhancing decision-making efficiency and better understanding of social trends.

X. Pan et al. (Eds.): ICCC 2023, LNCS 14207, pp. 100–115, 2024.
https://doi.org/10.1007/978-3-031-51671-9_8

Text sentiment analysis is a natural language processing technique that categorizes the sentiment polarity expressed in the text and is commonly used for analyzing emotions in social media [4, 5]. In recent years, the development of deep learning technology has led to significant advancements in sentiment analysis. By utilizing deep learning models, sentiment polarity within the text can be accurately identified, resulting in precise classification outcomes [6]. However, research on sentiment analysis specifically tailored to Ethereum transactions is still in its early stages, and there is a significant lack of studies focusing on sentiment analysis of Chinese-language public opinions on the Ethereum blockchain. Therefore, this paper aims to design a deep learning-based Ethereum Chinese sentiment analysis model to assist Ethereum participants and users in understanding market sentiment and investor emotions, thereby improving decision-making efficiency. Additionally, it will contribute to the establishment of measures for sentiment regulation and monitoring within the Ethereum ecosystem.

This research aims to design a deep learning-based Ethereum Chinese sentiment classification model, covering aspects such as related work on Ethereum and sentiment analysis, model design, experimental setup, results analysis, and conclusions. The study makes the following contributions:

Data Extraction and Compilation: This study extracted and compiled a real dataset containing Chinese Ethereum transactions, providing valuable input data for sentiment analysis.

Chinese Sentiment Analysis on Ethereum Transactions: The study proposes a comprehensive and effective model specifically tailored to handle sentiment analysis tasks on Chinese-language Ethereum transactions.

By addressing the challenges of sentiment analysis in the context of Ethereum transactions, this research contributes to the advancement of sentiment analysis techniques applied to blockchain data. It allows for a deeper understanding of the emotions and sentiments present within the Ethereum community, aiding Ethereum participants and researchers in making informed decisions and regulatory measures.

2 Related Work

2.1 Public Opinion Analysis Technology

Public opinion analysis is a process of systematically collecting, collating and analyzing public opinions, attitudes and opinions. Sentiment analysis is a key task of public opinion analysis, and its goal is to identify and classify the emotional tendencies of texts, including positive, negative and neutral sentiments. Understanding public sentiment is critical for companies to improve their products, governments to improve policies, and media to report on them.

Sentiment analysis is an algorithm used to classify or score the emotions expressed in text. Common sentiment analysis models include:

- Lexicon-based approaches: These methods utilize sentiment dictionaries [7] and statistical rules [8] to determine the sentiment of the text based on the presence of specific sentiment words.

- Traditional machine learning methods: Such as Naive Bayes, Support Vector Machines [9], which use a set of handcrafted features to predict the sentiment of the text.
- Deep learning methods: These include Recurrent Neural Networks (RNN) [10], Convolutional Neural Networks (CNN) [11], and Long Short-Term Memory Networks (LSTM) [12]. Deep learning models can automatically learn features from the input data, making them effective for capturing complex patterns in text and improving sentiment analysis accuracy.

Lexicon-based methods use unsupervised training, which makes them simple, fast, and scalable. However, this also means that these methods heavily rely on the sentiment dictionary, leading to lower accuracy compared to supervised machine learning methods [13]. Another issue with lexicon-based approaches is their domain dependency, making them less suitable for domains without specific sentiment dictionaries.

Traditional machine learning methods, on the other hand, utilize supervised training and can achieve higher performance [14]. However, these supervised methods require a substantial amount of training data and have slower training speeds, resulting in a significant time investment.

In recent years, deep learning-based sentiment analysis methods have shown remarkable effectiveness [15]. By providing raw data to deep learning models, these methods can automatically detect potential sentiment representations and process them accordingly. Long Short-Term Memory (LSTM) is widely used in sentiment analysis tasks as it can incorporate both the context of the text and analyze emotions [16].For instance, in 2016, Xu et al. proposed a Cache-based Long Short-Term Memory Network (CLSTM) [17], which introduces a cache mechanism to capture the semantics of long texts by incorporating cache into units with different forget rates. Additionally, in 2018, Rao et al. presented a Sentence Representation LSTM (SR-LSTM) for document-level sentiment classification [18]. The first step involves transforming the document into sentence vectors through word embeddings, and the second step uses these sentence vectors as inputs to obtain the document representation. Moreover, in 2022, Onan et al. introduced a Group Enhancement Mechanism for Bidirectional Convolutional Recurrent Neural Networks (BiCRNN-GE) [19]. This structure groups Bidirectional LSTM and Bidirectional Gated Recurrent Unit (GRU) to extract contextual information from the text. The Bidirectional LSTM considers both forward and backward context information simultaneously, while the GRU utilizes gate mechanisms to control information flow, effectively capturing long-term dependencies.

Attention mechanisms have been used to enhance the learning capabilities of deep learning models and improve the accuracy of classification [20] For instance, in 2016, Zhou et al. proposed using an attention mechanism to enhance bilingual representation models, highlighting sentences with strong emotions [21]. In 2018, He et al. introduced an attention-based LSTM model for document-level sentiment analysis and discovered two methods for transferring knowledge from document-level data, which effectively improved the performance of aspect-level sentiment classification at a lower cost [22]. Furthermore, in 2021, Basiri et al. proposed an Attention-Based CNN-RNN Deep Model

(ABCDM) [20], which uses attention mechanisms to reduce the dimensionality of features and extract local features. This approach aims to enhance the model's ability to focus on relevant information and improve its performance in sentiment analysis tasks.

2.2 Ethereum Data Analysis

With the rapid development of Ethereum, an increasing amount of research is focusing on how to analyze and mine Ethereum blockchain data [26]. Ethereum transaction texts exhibit a high degree of flexibility and diversity, as they can execute various smart contract operations. Consequently, their features and distribution throughout the Ethereum network are remarkably extensive and complex. Transaction text in Ethereum transactions consists of a string composed of hexadecimal characters. Each character represents 4 bits (one hexadecimal digit corresponds to a 4-bit binary number). Typically, this string begins with '0x' and represents a series of hexadecimal numbers. The initial characters usually contain the function's signature, which is a unique string identifying the function to be executed. Subsequent characters contain the function's parameter data, which is the hexadecimal representation of the input parameters for the function. Additionally, the text's length may vary from one transaction to another, depending on the function being called and the number and type of its parameters.

The content distribution of transaction texts is highly diverse due to the varying functions and parameters of different smart contracts, making it widespread throughout the Ethereum network. Some common transaction texts include transfers, token exchanges, smart contract creation, and invocation of smart contract functions. These operations typically constitute the majority of the distribution of transaction texts. Additionally, certain transaction texts are entirely custom, enabling customized smart contract operations to perform various functions such as voting, auctions, gaming, or social sentiment discussions. These types of textual content can reflect users' opinions and emotions, while also warranting caution regarding potential malicious activities or harmful behaviors, such as spreading false information, malicious attacks, privacy breaches, and social opinion manipulation.

In this study, a collection and organization of such custom content were performed, resulting in 125,941 transaction records collected from the Ethereum blockchain, all containing Chinese textual information. Furthermore, an analysis of specific Ethereum transaction texts was conducted, with the results shown in Fig. 1.

An Ethereum transaction consists of three parts: metadata, nonce, and data. Data refers to the transaction's payload, which originates from sending, calling, or deploying smart contracts on the Ethereum network [3]. Therefore, there are two types of transactions that can be executed on Ethereum:

- Transactions not interacting with contracts: These transactions involve sending ETH directly from an External Owned Account (EOA), commonly referred to as a wallet address, to another EOA. In these cases, the payload is typically empty (0x). For example, the payload for a transaction with the hash "0x909d79ad5564b23bdc1aef4348aeb1a2e2ed57debbf734338aa8268146cfcb6d" is"x". When users initiate direct transfer transactions, they can provide additional information through text or form fields by using wallet software, exchange platforms, or development tools. This input data will be

Fig. 1. Data word cloud.

stored in the transaction's data. For instance, a transaction with the hash "0x9ac5a4562016f507d8060873dcb9c8f02917ad73c99dec0dfe19cfd78662e9d3" contains some user-inputted text information.

- Transactions interacting with contracts: The majority of transactions involve external accounts interacting with smart contracts. Most contracts are written in Solidity, and their interactions follow the Application Binary Interface (ABI). The payload generated by the transaction stores the first eight bytes of the Keccak-256 [27, 28] hash of the function called within the contract, as well as the contract's address. For example, in a transaction with the hash 0xd0dcbe007569fcfa1902dae0ab8b4e078efe42e231786312289b1eee5590f6a1, the payload content is "0xa9059cbb0000000000000000000000004f6742badb0 49791cd9a37ea913f2bac38d0127900000000000000000000000000000000000000 00000000000000000003b0559f4". The "a9059cbb" represents the hash value of the function name and parameters used to specify the function to be called. According to the ABI specification, integer values (such as addresses, which are 20-byte integers) are displayed as 32-byte words in the ABI, padded with leading zeros. So, we know that the recipient address for this transaction is "0x4f6742badb049791cd9a37ea913f2bac38d01279" and the transaction amount is "3b0559f4" [36].

3 The MABLSTM Sentiment Analysis Model

The MABLSTM sentiment analysis model is primarily divided into two parts: data preprocessing and sentiment analysis model. In the first stage, Ethereum raw data is collected, cleaned, encoded, and filtered to obtain key text. In the second stage, the Ethereum transaction text's feature representation is acquired, followed by feature extraction using BLSTM. Subsequently, a multi-head attention mechanism is employed to determine the importance of different types of words. Finally, the data is passed through fully connected layers to obtain classification results.

3.1 Data Preprocessing

The most common methods for collecting Ethereum transaction data include synchronizing and querying data using Ethereum full nodes or utilizing official Ethereum API interfaces to obtain specific data. This data may encompass transaction records, smart contract invocation records, contract deployment records, and blockchain state, among other information [26].

We deployed an Ethereum full node to obtain the complete set of transaction data and used the Ethereum ETL tool [30] to export Ethereum raw transaction data to our local environment. Subsequently, we organized the raw transaction data based on the types of Ethereum transaction data.

Ethereum transaction data cannot be directly used for sentiment analysis, so data preprocessing is necessary to extract the required textual information. The preprocessing steps can include the following:

- Remove empty transaction data: Eliminate transactions in the dataset where the "Input data" column is equal to "0x".
- Remove smart contract call and deployment transaction data: Function calls in Ethereum Virtual Machine are specified by the first four bytes of the data sent with the transaction. These 4-byte signatures are defined as the first four bytes of the Keccak hash (SHA3) of the function signature. The data from the input data column of each transaction is identified using Ethereum Signature Database [35] to remove smart contract call and deployment transaction data.
- Remove transcoding gibberish data: The Input data in Ethereum transactions is stored in hexadecimal format, and when converting hexadecimal to UTF-8, some Chinese content may appear as gibberish.
- Remove stop words: Remove common stop words such as "的" (of), "是" (is/am/are/be), "在" (in), etc., as they often lack explicit sentiment orientation in sentiment analysis.
- Text cleaning: Remove special characters, punctuation marks, etc., from the text to maintain data cleanliness and consistency.

After completing the above data collection and preprocessing steps, we obtain a suitable Ethereum-related dataset for sentiment analysis.

3.2 Sentiment Analysis Model

In this study, we enhance the accuracy of sentiment analysis by using a multi-head attention mechanism to increase the weight of common sentiment words while giving special weighting to some unique terms found on the blockchain. The main components of our sentiment analysis model are divided into five layers: the input layer, embedding layer, BLSTM layer, multi-head attention layer, and fully connected layer, as illustrated in Fig. 2.

Input Layer: The input layer is responsible for generating input samples of preprocessed text. The input text is represented as: $\{x_1, x_2, x_3, ..., x_i, ..., x_m\}$, where x_i is the ith word in the text, and m represents the size of the input text.

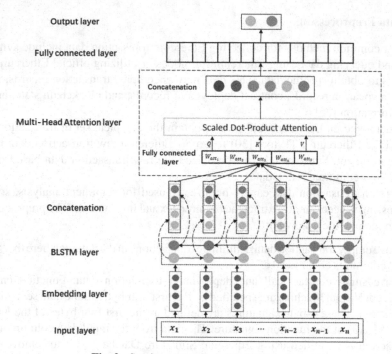

Fig. 2. Sentiment Analysis Model Structure.

BLSTM Layer: Long Short-Term Memory (LSTM) is a special type of recurrent neural network (RNN) designed for handling sequential data. Traditional RNNs suffer from vanishing and exploding gradients, making them difficult to capture long-term dependencies. LSTM was introduced to address these issues by incorporating gate mechanisms into the basic RNN architecture [20].

- Input gate (i_t): Determines which information will be added to the cell state.
- Forget Gate (f_t): Determines which information will be forgotten from the cell state.
- Output gate (o_t): Determines which information from the cell state will be output to the current time step's hidden state, serving as the current time step's output.

By using these gate mechanisms, LSTM can effectively learn long-term dependencies, enabling better handling of long sequential data.

Let $\sigma(.)$, $\tanh(.)$, and $\odot$ represent the sigmoid function, tanh function, and element-wise multiplication, respectively.

x_t and h_t are the input vector and hidden state vector at time t, respectively. U and W are weight matrices from the input layer to the hidden layer, and b is the bias vector. The output of the forget gate is a number in the range [0, 1] that determines which information needs to be forgotten [20].

$$f_t = \sigma(W_f h_{t-1} + U_f x_t + b_f) \tag{1}$$

The input gate calculates i_t to and $\tilde{c}_t$ using the following formulas to determine the new information that the cell unit needs to store at time t:

$$i_t = \sigma(W_i h_{t-1} + U_i x_t + b_i) \tag{2}$$

$$\tilde{c}_t = \tanh(W_c h_{t-1} + U_c x_t + b_c) \tag{3}$$

$$c_t = f_t \odot c_{t-1} + i_t \odot \tilde{c}_t \tag{4}$$

The output gate calculates the part of the cell unit that needs to be output using the following formula:

$$o_t = \sigma(W_o h_{t-1} + U_o x_t + b_o) \tag{5}$$

$$h_t = o_t \odot \tanh(c_t) \tag{6}$$

BLSTM (Bidirectional Long Short-Term Memory) is a variation of LSTM that combines both forward $\overrightarrow{h_t}$ and backward $\overleftarrow{h_t}$ hidden layers, allowing BLSTM to utilize both past and future context to predict the current sentiment [23, 24]. The formula for BLSTM is as follows:

$$h_i = \left[\overrightarrow{h_t} \oplus \overleftarrow{h_t} \right] \tag{7}$$

$$\overrightarrow{h_t} = \overrightarrow{\text{LSTM}}(W_t, \overrightarrow{h_{t-1}}, C_{t-1}) \tag{8}$$

$$\overleftarrow{h_t} = \overleftarrow{\text{LSTM}}(W_t, \overleftarrow{h_{t-1}}, C_{t-1}) \tag{9}$$

Finally, we obtain the output of the entire sentence as $\{h_1, h_2, h_3, ..., h_i, ..., h_m\}$, where h_i represents the output of the BLSTM layer.

Attention Layer: The attention mechanism [25] is used to automatically select and focus on key information within the text. It allows the model to weight sentiment words during text processing, enabling better capturing of the sentiment polarity within the text. The process of attention mechanism is illustrated in Fig. 3. The computation of attention involves three steps. In the first step, attention weights are calculated. This paper utilizes an additive model to compute the correlation between the input sequence $\{h_1, h_2, ..., h_i, ..., h_m\}$ and the query vector q_{att}, resulting in a correlation queue $\{e_1, e_2, ..., e_t\}$ between q_{att} and each input h_i. The second step involves normalization, where the weighted queue is normalized using the softmax function, yielding the attention distribution $\{y_1, y_2, ..., y_t\}$ for the query vector q_{att} on the input sequence h_i. The third step computes attention by performing a weighted sum of the input sequence based on the attention distribution y_t. The formula is as follows:

$$e_t = \tanh(A_{att} * h_i + b_{att}) \tag{10}$$

$$y_t = \text{softmax}(e_t) \tag{11}$$

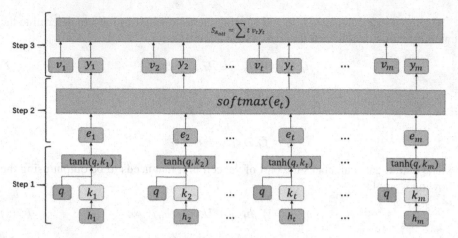

Fig. 3. Attention Mechanism Flowchart.

$$S_{A_{att}} = \sum_t y_t h_t \qquad (12)$$

h_i is as shown in formula 7, softmax(.) represents the softmax function. A_{att} is the weight matrix of the attention mechanism, and $S_{A_{att}}$ represents the context vector after being weighted by the attention mechanism weight matrix.

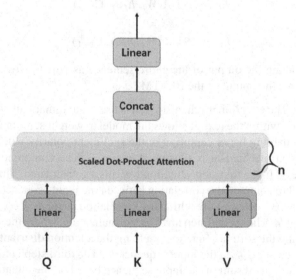

Fig. 4. Multi-head Attention Mechanism Model.

The multi-head attention mechanism [34] (refer to Fig. 4) introduces multiple attention heads, each utilizing multiple query vectors $Q = \{q_1, q_2, ..., q_n\}$, to learn different attention weights from input information $(K, V) = \{(k_1, v_1), (k_2, v_2), ..., (k_t, v_t)\}$. This allows the model to simultaneously focus on different positions and semantic information. The linear transformation formulas for obtaining the query queue $Q = \{q_1, q_2, ..., q_n\}$ and input information $(K, V) = \{(k_1, v_1), (k_2, v_2), ..., (k_t, v_t)\}$ are as follows:

$$Q = W_Q x_i \tag{13}$$

$$K = W_K x_i \tag{14}$$

$$V = W_V x_i \tag{15}$$

where $K = V = \{h_1, h_2, ..., h_i, ..., h_m\}$, W_Q, W_K and W_V is the weight matrix.
The calculation of attention weights for each attention head is as follows:

$$A_i = softmax(\frac{QK^T}{sqrt(d_k)}) \tag{16}$$

$$S_i = \sum_t A_i V \tag{17}$$

d_k represents the dimension of the key vector, and sqrt(.) denotes the square root function, S_i represents the attention output vector computed by the query vector q_i.
$$S = S_1 \oplus S_2 \oplus ... \oplus S_n$$
Where $\oplus$ denotes the vector concatenation operation.

Fully Connected Layer: Maps the representation vectors to the label space for relationship classification. The fully connected layer maps the learned features to specific relationship categories and generates the prediction results.

By combining BLSTM with the multi-head attention mechanism, this model can fully utilize the contextual information in the text data to automatically learn important information relevant to sentiment analysis tasks.

4 Experimental Setup and Result Analysis

4.1 Experimental Setup

This section will provide a detailed explanation of the experimental setup, including the experimental data, evaluation metrics, and result analysis.

Experimental Data. The experimental data for this study is collected from real Chinese text data in Ethereum transaction data, as shown in Table 1.

After performing data cleaning and preprocessing on the Chinese data from Ethereum transactions, we obtained the experimental dataset for this study. Each data entry is labeled with a sentiment category: positive or negative. To ensure the reliability and representativeness of the experiments, we used 60% of the data as the training set, 20% as the test set, and 20% as the validation set.

Table 1. Details of the Datasets Used in This Study.

Dataset	Ethereum transaction data
Target Series	Ethereum
Related series	Chinese text information
Time	2015/8/7–2021/7/15
The amount of data	125941
Train/Validation/Test	75565/25188/25188

Model Evaluation Metrics. Three evaluation metrics, namely Accuracy, Recall, and $F1$-score , are used to assess the performance of the system in sentiment analysis tasks. These metrics are widely used in sentiment analysis tasks [33]. The formulas for calculating these metrics are shown below:

$$\textbf{accuracy} = \frac{TP+TN}{TP+TN+FP+FN}$$

$$\textbf{precision} = \frac{TP}{TP+FP}$$

$$\textbf{recall} = \frac{TP}{TP+FN}$$

$$\textbf{F}_1 - \textbf{score} = \frac{2*precision*recall}{precision+recall}$$

The meanings of TP, TN, FP, and FN are shown in Table 2.

Table 2. Parameter Meaning.

	Actual		
Predicted		Positive	Negative
	Positive	True Positive (TP)	False Positive (FP)
	Negative	False Negative (FN)	True Negative (TN)

Parameter Configuration. During the training process, this model requires the configuration and fine-tuning of many parameters to achieve the best classification performance.

The training batch size is set to 128, and a dropout rate of 0.2 is used to prevent overfitting. L2 regularization is applied to control the model's complexity. The Adam optimizer is utilized with a learning rate set at 10^{-4}, and backpropagation is employed for network training. Cross-entropy is chosen as the loss function, and accuracy is computed to assess the model's convergence. The number of heads in the multi-head attention mechanism is set at 8 to optimize the model's performance and attention capture. Some of the model's parameter settings are shown in Table 3.

Table 3. Parameter Settings.

Batch size	Units	Epochs	learning Rate
128	128	64	0.0001

4.2 Comparative Experiment

We compared MABLSTM with the following baseline to confirm the effectiveness of the multi-head attention mechanism in sentiment analysis in the Ethereum-related domain:

ABCDM: Attention-based Bidirectional CNN-RNN Deep Model. In this model, each branch (BLSTM branch and BGRU branch) independently employs two parallel convolutional layers with different kernel sizes for convolution in the convolutional layer.

ABLSTM: This approach uses traditional attention mechanisms that only increase the weight of sentiment words, without considering the impact of specific nouns on sentiment analysis.

SVM: SVM is one of the commonly used benchmark models for sentiment classification. In this experiment, a linear kernel SVM with a penalty parameter (C) set to 1 is employed.

CNN: CNN is another frequently used model in sentiment classification. It is capable of handling relatively complex data. In our experiment, we combine the CNN model with word embeddings to achieve sentiment analysis.

4.3 Experimental Result

After conducting benchmark tests on ABCDM, ABLSTM, SVM and CNN, Table 4 displays the evaluation metrics, including *Accuracy*, *Recall* and F_1-**score**, for the MABLSTM model and the three aforementioned models on the Ethereum transaction dataset.

Table 4. Table captions should be placed above the tables.

Evaluation Indicators	Accuracy	Recall	F_1-score
CNN	63.19%	70.10%	64.70%
SVM	66.85%	74.46%	71.79%
ABLSTM	69.55%	73.57%	67.76%
ABCDM	66.82%	67.87%	65.44%
MABLSTM	71.75%	77.18%	71.01%

The experimental results indicate that SVM and CNN, as traditional sentiment analysis models, achieved good results in the Ethereum text classification task with accuracies of 66.84% and 63.19%, respectively. The accuracy of the BLSTM model incorporating traditional attention mechanism was only 69.55%, while the accuracy of the ABCDM model, which concatenates the BLSTM branch and BGRU branch, was even lower at 66.82%. In contrast, the MABLSTM model achieved an accuracy of 71.75% in this comparative experiment. The reason lies in the fact that MABLSTM enhances the weight of proper nouns, leading to more accurate classification results. Regarding categories, the MABLSTM model demonstrated the highest recall and F1-score values, second only to the SVM classifier. This proves the effectiveness and superiority of the multi-head attention mechanism combined with BLSTM in sentiment analysis of Ethereum transaction texts.

The selection of the number of heads for the multi-head attention mechanism: To assess the impact of the number of heads on the experimental results, this experiment conducted statistical analysis on the accuracy of the attention mechanism with different numbers of heads (as shown in Fig. 5). The experimental range for 'Head Numbers' was from 6 to 12. From the experimental results, it can be observed that as ' Head Numbers ' increases, the model performance continuously improves. Subsequently, as the number of heads further increases, the model performance stabilizes. Therefore, when the value of ' Head Numbers ' is set to 8, the accuracy is optimal. Hence, in this experiment, the number of heads for the multi-head attention mechanism is set to 8.

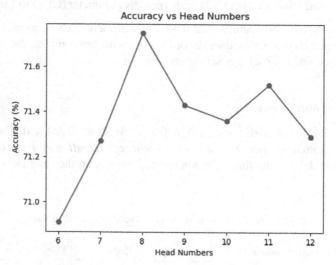

Fig. 5. The accuracy for different 'headNum's.

5   Conclusion and Outlook

5.1   Conclusion

This study proposes a sentiment analysis model for Ethereum transaction information. The experimental results demonstrate that the model achieves good performance on the Ethereum transaction dataset. Accurately capturing users' sentiment and market sentiment can not only assist in Ethereum regulation but also provide more valuable information for users.

Furthermore, our model has several important advantages and contributions in sentiment analysis of Chinese text data from Ethereum transactions. Firstly, our model adopts the MABLSTM deep learning architecture, where the bidirectional LSTM structure comprehensively considers the contextual information from both past and future text flows. The attention mechanism enhances the importance of sentiment words and blockchain-specific keywords in the text, thus improving the accuracy and stability of sentiment classification. Secondly, our model is trained to automatically learn specific sentiment patterns and associations in Ethereum transactions, which may enhance its generalization and performance in other blockchain sentiment analysis tasks.

5.2 Outlook

Although our model has achieved satisfactory results in sentiment analysis of Chinese text data from Ethereum transactions, there are still aspects that can be further improved and explored.

Firstly, we can consider introducing more semantic features and contextual information to enhance the model's understanding of sentiment analysis tasks. For example, exploring the use of word embeddings, syntactic analysis, and other techniques to enrich text representations.

Secondly, we can expand the size of the dataset to improve the model's generalization ability. By collecting more Ethereum transaction data, including different types of transactions and more contextual information, we can comprehensively evaluate the model's performance.

Moreover, we can further explore the interpretability and explainability of the model. In-depth research into the model's decision-making process and key features in the sentiment classification process can enhance people's understanding and trust in the model's results.

Lastly, we can apply the model to sentiment analysis tasks in other domains, such as internet news sentiment analysis. By verifying the performance and adaptability of the model in different domains, we can expand its application scope and practical use cases.

In conclusion, the attention-based bidirectional long short-term memory network model shows great potential in sentiment analysis of Chinese text data from Ethereum transactions. Through continuous research and improvement, we can further enhance the model's performance and adaptability, providing more accurate and reliable sentiment analysis tools for participants in the Ethereum market and offering deeper insights for Ethereum regulation and sentiment analysis.

References

1. Oliva, G.A., Hassan, A.E., Jiang, Z.M.: An exploratory study of smart contracts in the Ethereum blockchain platform. Empir. Softw. Eng. **25**, 1864–1904 (2020)
2. Kushwaha, S.S., Joshi, S., Singh, D., et al.: Ethereum smart contract analysis tools: a systematic review. IEEE Access **10**, 57037–57062 (2022)

3. Buterin, V.: A next-generation smart contract and decentralized application platform. White Paper **3**(37), 2–1 (2014)
4. Pang, Bo., Lee, L.: Opinion mining and sentiment analysis. Found. Trends® Inform. Retrieval **2**(1–2), 1–135 (2008). https://doi.org/10.1561/1500000011
5. Peng, H., Cambria, E., Hussain, A.: A review of sentiment analysis research in Chinese language. Cogn. Comput. **9**, 423–435 (2017)
6. Wang, Y., Zhu, J., Wang, Z., et al.: Review of applications of natural language processing in text sentiment analysis. J. Comput. Appl. **42**(4), 1011 (2022)
7. Taboada, M., Brooke, J., Tofiloski, M., et al.: Lexicon-based methods for sentiment analysis. Comput. Linguist. **37**(2), 267–307 (2011)
8. Turney, P.D., Littman, M.L.: Measuring praise and criticism: Inference of semantic orientation from association. ACM Trans. Inform. Syst. **21**(4), 315–346 (2003)
9. Pang, B., Lee, L., Vaithyanathan, S.: Thumbs up? Sentiment classification using machine learning techniques. arXiv preprint arXiv:cs/0205070 (2002)
10. Mikolov, T., Karafiát, M., Burget, L. et al.: Recurrent neural network based language model. In: Interspeech, vol. 2, no. 3, pp. 1045–1048 (2010)
11. Kim, Y.: Convolutional neural networks for sentence classification. Eprint Arxiv. arXiv preprint arXiv:1408.5882 (2014)
12. Hochreiter, S., Schmidhuber, J.: Long short-term memory. Neural Comput. **9**(8), 1735–1780 (1997)
13. Basiri, M.E., Kabiri, A.: HOMPer: a new hybrid system for opinion mining in the Persian language. J. Inf. Sci. **46**(1), 101–117 (2020)
14. Basiri, M.E., Kabiri, A.: Words are important: improving sentiment analysis in the persian language by lexicon refining. ACM Trans. Asian Low-resource Lang. Inform. Process. (TALLIP) **17**(4), 1–18 (2018)
15. Li, J., Sun, A., Han, J., et al.: A survey on deep learning for named entity recognition. IEEE Trans. Knowl. Data Eng. **34**(1), 50–70 (2020)
16. Minaee, S., Kalchbrenner, N., Cambria, E., et al.: Deep learning–based text classification: a comprehensive review. ACM Comput. Surv. (CSUR) **54**(3), 1–40 (2021)
17. Xu, J., Chen, D., Qiu, X., et al.: Cached long short-term memory neural networks for document-level sentiment classification. arXiv preprint arXiv:1610.04989 (2016)
18. Rao, G., Huang, W., Feng, Z., et al.: LSTM with sentence representations for document-level sentiment classification. Neurocomputing **308**, 49–57 (2018)
19. Onan, A.: Bidirectional convolutional recurrent neural network architecture with group-wise enhancement mechanism for text sentiment classification. J. King Saud Univ.-Comput. Inform. Sci. **34**(5), 2098–2117 (2022)
20. Basiri, M.E., Nemati, S., Abdar, M., et al.: ABCDM: an attention-based bidirectional CNN-RNN deep model for sentiment analysis. Future Gener. Comput. Syst. **115**, 279–294 (2021)
21. Zhou, X., Wan, X., Xiao, J.: Attention-based LSTM network for cross-lingual sentiment classification. In: Proceedings of the 2016 Conference on Empirical Methods in Natural Language Processing, pp. 247–256 (2016)
22. He, R., Lee, W.S., Ng, H.T., et al.: Exploiting document knowledge for aspect-level sentiment classification. arXiv preprint arXiv:1806.04346 (2018)
23. Zhou, P., Shi, W., Tian, J., et al.: Attention-based bidirectional long short-term memory networks for relation classification. In: Proceedings of the 54th Annual Meeting of the Association for Computational Linguistics, vol. 2: Short papers, pp. 207–212 (2016)
24. Zhang, D., Wang, D.: Relation classification via recurrent neural network. arXiv preprint arXiv:1508.01006 (2015)
25. Bahdanau, D., Cho, K., Bengio, Y.: Neural machine translation by jointly learning to align and translate. arXiv preprint arXiv:1409.0473 (2014)

26. Zheng, P., Zheng, Z., Wu, J., et al.: Xblock -eth: extracting and exploring blockchain data from ethereum. IEEE Open J. Comput. Soc. **1**, 95–106 (2020)
27. Bertoni, G., Daemen, J., Peeters, M., et al.: The keccak SHA-3 submission. Submission to NIST (Round 3) **6**(7), 16 (2011)
28. Wood, G., Ethereum: a secure decentralized generalized transaction ledger Berlin version (2020)
29. Antonopoulos, A.M., Wood, G.: Mastering Ethereum : Building Smart Contracts and Dapps. O'reilly Media, Sebastopol (2018)
30. Evgeny, M.: The D5 team. Ethereum ETL (2018). https://github.com/blockchain-etl/ethere um-etl
31. ethereum.org. Transactions (2023). https://ethereum.org/en/developers/docs/transactions/
32. Mikolov, T., Chen, K., Corrado, G., et al.: Efficient estimation of word representations in vector space. arXiv preprint arXiv:1301.3781 (2013)
33. Liu, B.: Sentiment Analysis: Mining Opinions, Sentiments, and Emotions. Cambridge University Press, Cambridge (2020)
34. Vaswani, A., Shazeer, N., Parmar, N., et al.: Attention is all you need. In: Advances in Neural Information Processing Systems, vol. 30 (2017)
35. Ethereum signature database. API documentation 2018. https://www.4byte.directory/docs/
36. ethereum.org. Contract ABI specification (2023). https://docs.soliditylang.org/en/v0.8.22/ abi-spec.html

Prompt Tuning Models on Sentiment-Aware for Explainable Recommendation

Xiuhua Long and Ting Jin[✉]

School of Computer Science and Technology, Hainan University, Haikou 570228, China
jinting@hainanu.edu.cn

Abstract. Explainable recommendation systems primarily utilize users' ratings and corresponding reviews to make recommendations and generate meaningful explanations. However, most explainable recommendation methods only consider one aspect of sentiment in the reviews and lack sufficient exploration of the review texts. Besides, these methods often rely on deep neural networks and do not adequately consider how to effectively integrate extracted information into the pre-trained model to improve the quality of explanation text. In this work, we propose SAPER, which is the first end-to-end framework that combines sentiment analysis and prompt learning in explainable recommendations. For the rating prediction task, we employ multi-granularity sentiment analysis, simultaneously incorporating coarse-grained and fine-grained information from review texts to capture user preferences and item characteristics. For the explanation generation task, we design a multi-level approach that integrates user and item IDs, as well as rating information, as soft prompts into the pre-trained model to generate personalized explanations. Experimental results demonstrate that our model outperforms state-of-the-art baseline models on three datasets. In particular, we validate the effectiveness of multi-granularity sentiment analysis and soft prompt strategies. Experimental analysis indicates that the recommendation explanations generated by the SAPER model are semantically closer to actual reviews.

Keywords: Explainable Recommendation · Sentiment Analysis · Soft Prompts · Pre-trained Models · Joint Learning

1 Introduction

With the rapid development of the Internet, information overload has become increasingly serious. Recommender systems play a crucial role in alleviating information overload issues. They can provide personalized recommendations by modeling user preferences based on historical interactions between users and items. However, it remains challenging to provide a reasonable explanation while recommending the results to the user. The interpretability of recommender systems is especially necessary, as it can enhance user satisfaction, improve recommendation accuracy, and help users make better decisions [1].

© The Author(s), under exclusive license to Springer Nature Switzerland AG 2024
X. Pan et al. (Eds.): ICCC 2023, LNCS 14207, pp. 116–132, 2024.
https://doi.org/10.1007/978-3-031-51671-9_9

Collaborative Filtering (CF) is one of the classic models in recommendation systems. Traditional CF approaches are implemented through matrix factorization [2] (MF) algorithms. These algorithms typically utilize user-item ratings as their training data. Besides, they also lead to some issues, such as cold-start, data sparsity, and uninterpretable problem. Using textual reviews can effectively alleviate the issues. These reviews contain a wealth of latent information. By performing sentiment analysis on review texts, we can better understand user preferences and item characteristics.

Currently, mainstream sentiment analysis methods [3] primarily focus on two levels: coarse-grained and fine-grained. Coarse-grained sentiment analysis involves determining the overall sentiment polarity of text at the sentence level. Fine-grained sentiment analysis involves a detailed examination at the word or aspect level. However, sentiment analysis based solely on one granularity level is unable to capture user interests accurately and comprehensively.

In addition, traditional recommendation systems have focused excessively on the accuracy of recommendation results, and often neglect the interpretability of recommendations. Explainable recommendations have been getting more and more attention [4], but they also face some limitations, such as the lack of benchmark explanation text. Most current research treats interpretability in recommendation systems as an auxiliary subtask, and there is no approach to do a quantitative evaluation of explainable recommendations.

In this paper, we propose a novel sentiment-aware hybrid recommendation framework named Prompt Tuning Models on Sentiment-Aware for Explainable Recommendation (SAPER). It is designed to comprehensively consider rating prediction and explanation generation to improve recommendation performance and explanation quality. In the rating prediction task, we leverage Latent Dirichlet Allocation (LDA) topic modeling and syntactic analysis to extract features of varying granularity from reviews. In the explanation generation task, we adopt prompt learning methods to integrate user and item IDs, rating-level, and review-level information into the pre-trained language model, which facilitates to generate recommendation justifications and enhances model interpretability.

Our main contributions can be summarized as follows:

(1) We propose a joint learning framework based on rating prediction and explanation generation. To the best of our knowledge, we are the first to simultaneously integrate prompt learning and sentiment analysis into explainable recommendations.
(2) We develop a sentiment-based recommendation model, which simultaneously integrates coarse-grained and fine-grained sentiment from review texts, effectively capturing user preferences and item characteristics.
(3) We design a multi-level explanation generation method using soft prompt learning. This method incorporates user and item ids, along with rating information, as prompts directly into the pre-trained model.
(4) Experimental results illustrate that our model achieves better performance than other state-of-the-art models on three datasets.

2 Related Work

2.1 Review-Based Rating Prediction

Early review-based recommendation systems primarily utilize topic models to learn semantic features of users and items. HFT [5] and CTR [6] extracted review features using LDA models, which were then integrated into MF frameworks to infer latent topics. However, traditional topic model approaches are often based on bag-of-words models, neglecting word order and contextual information, which lead to semantic losses.

With the success of deep learning in natural language processing, many studies have attempted to combine deep neural networks with CF to improve recommendation performance. ConvMF [7] utilizes CNN and probabilistic matrix factorization to learn semantic information from review text, aiming to obtain latent semantic representations of reviews. DeepCoNN [8] is the first model to model users and items using neural networks from reviews jointly. It employs two parallel CNN networks to extract semantic features from user reviews and item reviews separately. NARRE [9] utilizes an attention mechanism to select relevant information for rating prediction.

While recommendation performance has significantly improved, these efforts have only focused on the static extraction of user and item feature vectors. They tend to overlook the dynamic interactions between users and items, and often lack precise comprehension of textual reviews.

2.2 Sentiment-Based Recommendation

In the field of e-commerce, recommendation systems and sentiment analysis techniques both focus on extracting user preferences from reviews. The former concentrates on improving recommendation accuracy by utilizing user and item review information, while the latter assesses user sentiment tendencies by analyzing review texts.

Some research aims to integrate sentiment analysis of user reviews into recommendations. At a fine-grained level, Pham et al. [10] proposed an aspect-based sentiment analysis model. They automatically identified words related to aspects through an attention mechanism and learned embeddings for each word. Hoang et al. [11] conducted a more detailed analysis of aspects and sentiment within the text, employing the BERT model for modeling and prediction. At a coarse-grained level, Yang et al. [12] introduced a sentence-level sentiment analysis approach, using a novel voting mechanism to generate recommendations. Additionally, conducting sentiment analysis at a single granularity level may not accurately capture user preferences. Some research attempts to combine cross-granularity sentiment analysis of user-item ratings and review texts to address data sparsity issues [13].

Previous work has shown that comprehensively considering emotions at different granularities can provide a more comprehensive and accurate representation of user preferences. Combining sentiment analysis of reviews with ratings can effectively enhance recommendation performance.

2.3 Explainable Recommendation

While deep neural networks have achieved significant advancements in recommendation systems, traditional models have not sufficiently considered the interpretability of recommendations. Many studies have improved the interpretability of recommendation systems by introducing attention mechanisms. D-Attn [14] combines global and local attention mechanisms to identify important words in review texts. CARL [15] uses CNN to capture word semantics and combines user-item interactions with review through the co-attention mechanism. In fact, these methods have certain limitations, as user reviews may not fully reflect the real attributes of items.

Some research employs RNN to generate explainable texts. These methods often adopt the encoder-decoder architecture. NRT [16] is the first model to simultaneously perform rating predictions and generating explanations. It uses MLP to encode users and items as embedding vectors, and subsequently employs GRU to generate abstract tips. Att2Seq [17] adopts a decoder built on two layers of LSTM.

Early research on explainable recommendations primarily relied on attention mechanisms and RNN, with insufficient exploration of pre-trained models and prompt learning [18, 19]. Li et al. [20] designed a personalized Transformer that utilizes user and item ids to generate corresponding explanations, effectively unifying the tasks of rating prediction and explanation generation. PEPLER [21] shifted the focus to effectively incorporating user and item ids into GPT-2 to facilitate the explanation generation. Existing researches indicate that introducing the pre-trained model can further enhance the accuracy and interpretability of recommendation systems [19, 22].

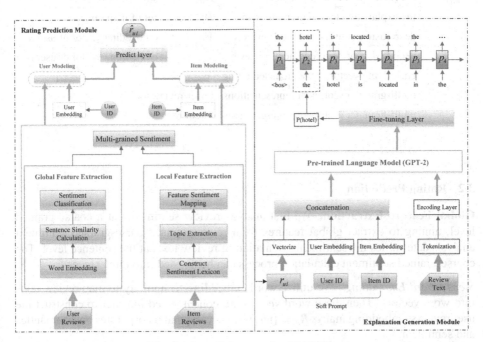

Fig. 1. Overall framework of SAPER.

3 Method

In this work, we propose a multi-task learning framework for explainable recommendation based on prompt learning and sentiment analysis. As shown in Fig. 1, SAPER consists of two modules: (a) rating prediction, which utilizes sentiment analysis to extract latent information from reviews, and then models interactions between users and items to predict ratings, (b) explanation generation, which simultaneously incorporates multi-level information as soft prompt into the pre-trained language model to generate explainable texts.

3.1 Problem Formulation

In the dataset T, each sample format is $(u, i, r_{(u,i)}, d_{(u,i)})$, our target is to predict the rating $\hat{r}_{(u,i)}$ and generate reasonable explanation $e_{(u,i)}$ based on the interactions of user u and item i. Table 1 defines the key symbols used in this paper.

Table 1. Notations

Symbol	Description	Symbol	Description
$r_{(u,i)}$	the real rating of user u to item i	M	number of users
$\hat{r}_{(u,i)}$	the predicted rating of user u to item i	N	number of items
$d_{(u,i)}$	the review text of user u to item i	D_u	set of user reviews
$e_{(u,i)}$	the explanation text of user u to item i	D_i	set of item reviews
φ_u	deep fusion of users and user' reviews	V_u	embedding vector of user u
φ_i	deep fusion of items and item' reviews	V_i	embedding vector of user i
V_r	embedding vector of the predicted rating		
Z_u	multi-granular sentiment representations of user reviews		
Z_i	multi-granular sentiment representations of item reviews		

3.2 Rating Prediction

Global Feature Extraction. We first analyze review sentiments at a coarse-grained level, aiming to extract global features from review texts. Coarse-grained sentiment analysis determines the sentiment orientation of review texts at the sentence level. The coarse-grained sentiment calculation process can be divided into three stages.

Step1: Word Embedding. We utilize word embedding technology to map review texts into word vectors. Then these word vectors are concatenated in order to construct the user reviews embedding matrix $R_u = [w_1, w_2, \cdots, w_t]$ that incorporates both semantics and sentiment.

Step2: Sentence Similarity Calculation. By performing operations on the review vector representations, it can calculate the semantic similarity between review texts and sentiment lexicons, thereby obtaining the probability of review sentiment polarity. The sentiment similarity of sentence level is computed as:

$$\alpha_{uj} = sim_{uj} = \frac{R_u \cdot G_j}{|R_u||G_j|} \tag{1}$$

$$\alpha_u = [\alpha_{u1}, \alpha_{u2}, \cdots \alpha_{uN}] \tag{2}$$

where α_{uj} is the similarity between user review embedding matrix R_u and words G_j in sentiment lexicon. By concatenating α_{uj}, we derive the overall sentiment similarity α_u.

$$p_u = \frac{\exp(\alpha_u)}{\sum_{j=1}^{N} \exp(\alpha_{uj})}, \ p_u \in (0, 1) \tag{3}$$

where p_u denotes the normalization pattern of user reviews similarity α_u.

Step3: Sentiment Classification. This module defines sentiment polarity analysis of texts as a binary classification task, which labels positive sentiments as 1 and negative sentiments as -1. Finally, we calculate a weighted sum of sentiment classification labels with the sentiment polarity probability matrix p_u.

$$C_u = \begin{cases} \sigma(S_u \cdot p_u), & \textit{if} \text{ positive} \\ 1 - \sigma(S_u \cdot p_u), & \textit{if} \text{ negative} \end{cases} \tag{4}$$

where σ represents the Sigmoid function, S_u is the sentiment classification label, C_u is the coarse-grained sentiment polarity of user review texts.

Local Feature Extraction. We utilize fine-grained sentiment analysis to extract local features from review texts. Fine-grained sentiment analysis determines the user's emotional tendency based on word-level or aspect-level information. The fine-grained sentiment calculation process is as follows.

Step1: Construct Sentiment Lexicon. We quantify feature words in review texts and their corresponding emotional levels through the sentiment lexicon. Each fine-grained feature is assigned a sentiment polarity value corresponding to five distinct states: very negative, moderately negative, neutral, moderately positive, and very positive. These states are described using the values $[-2, -1, 0, 1, 2]$ respectively.

Step2: Topic Information Extraction. This module utilizes the LDA model for topic clustering. Based on the document-topic distribution, user reviews D_u is segmented into multiple latent topics $T_u = \{T_{u1}, T_{u2}, \cdots, T_{uN}\}$. Then, we can obtain the feature words V_u for each topic through the topic-term distribution.

Step3: Feature Sentiment Mapping. We employ dependency syntax analysis for relationship extraction. By combining dependency relationships with grammatical tagging, we extract words from reviews that are more relevant to sentiment expression. Then, we introduce weight factors to identify keywords, and implement the mapping of feature words and sentiments.

Specifically, we firstly perform dependency syntax analysis individually from user reviews D_u. Next, we extract words with higher semantic importance as keywords, which allows us to obtain the representation of feature words V_u and sentiment words E_u of user reviews. Then, we map the feature-sentiment pair of user reviews, denoted as $\{V_u, E_u\}$. Finally, according to the sentiment lexicon, we construct fine-grained topic-sentiment matrices $F_u = [F_{u1}, F_{u2}, \cdots, F_{um}]$ of user reviews.

Deep Fusion and Prediction. This module jointly models both coarse-grained and fine-grained sentiment in review texts to extract multi-granular emotions, and obtain the final representations of review texts:

$$Z_u = \sum_{j=1}^{m} C_u \cdot F_{uj} \tag{5}$$

where Z_u represents the multi-granular sentiment representation of user reviews. Similarly, we can extract the multi-granular sentiment representation Z_i on item reviews.

We combine the latent feature vectors of users and items with sentiment representations extracted from review texts. For the user embedding M_u and item embedding N_i, we fuse them with their corresponding multi-granular sentiment representations through a feed-forward neural network, and then concatenate using an additive approach. The fusion process can be achieved by the following formula:

$$\varphi_u = (W_u Z_u + b_u) + M_u$$
$$\varphi_i = (W_i Z_i + b_i) + N_i \tag{6}$$
$$\varphi_{(u,i)} = [\varphi_u, \varphi_i]$$

where φ_u and φ_i respectively denote the initial fusion of users and items, $\varphi_{(u,i)}$ represents the deep fusion layer that concatenates φ_u and φ_i. Then, through a multi-layer feedforward neural network $H(\cdot)$ and activation function, the user-item interaction vector is computed as follows:

$$\phi_{(u,i)} = H(\varphi_{(u,i)}) = \sigma\left(W_L(\sigma(W_{L-1}(\cdots \sigma(W_1(\varphi_{(u,i)}) + b_1)\cdots) + b_{L-1})) + b_L\right) \tag{7}$$

where $H\left(\varphi_{(u,i)}\right)$ denotes a feedforward neural network with L layers, σ is the sigmoid activation function, W_L and b_L respectively represent the weight vector and bias of the L-th layer. Then, we predict the user's ratings for items:

$$\hat{r}_{(u,i)} = W^r \phi_{(u,i)} + b^r \tag{8}$$

During the model training process, in order to minimize the difference between predicted ratings and actual ratings, we select the Mean Squared Error loss function to measure the distance between ratings:

$$L_r = \frac{1}{\Omega} \sum_{(u,i)\in\Omega} \left(\hat{r}_{(u,i)} - r_{(u,i)}\right)^2 \tag{9}$$

where L_r is the loss on the rating prediction task, Ω represents a sample of the training set that user u interacts with item i.

3.3 Explanation Generation

Step 1: Constructing Soft Prompts. To obtain the optimal representation of soft prompts, we employ different methods for processing prompt information and natural language text. For the prompt information, we only consider essential information related to personalized explanation generation. Soft prompts typically consist of multiple prompt words that are interrelated. For the natural language text, we can directly obtain encoding representation through the encoding layer of pre-trained model.

Step 2: Fine-Tuning Pre-trained Models. The explanation generation task is modeled as a text generation task. To better utilize contextual information from user-item pair reviews, we have chosen to employ a pre-trained GPT-2 model for generating personalized explanation text. During the training phase, a fine-tuning layer is added on top of the pre-trained model, aiming to fix the parameters of the pre-trained model.

Step 3: Generating Predictive Sequences. Prompt fine-tuning formalizes the text generation task as a masked language model. We adopt an autoregressive masking mechanism, predicting the next word based on previously known words.

Specifically, each input sequence consists of a user id, an item id, a rating, and a review text. We encode user id, item id, and rating as soft prompts, and appended to the beginning of each review embedding.

$$I = [u, \ i, \ r_{(u,i)}, \ d_1, \ d_2, \ \cdots, \ d_{|G_{(u,i)}|}] \tag{10}$$

where $d_1, d_2, \cdots, d_{|G_{(u,i)}|}$ is the word sequence of review text. Next, we construct the soft prompt S, which is composed of user, item, and rating embedding vectors.

$$S = [V_u, \ V_i, \ V_r] \tag{11}$$

where V_u, V_i and V_r respectively denote the embedding vector of user u, item i and the predicted rating $\hat{r}_{(u,i)}$.

Subsequently, we feed soft prompt and review text embeddings into the pre-trained model, aiming to achieve personalized explanation text generation. Besides, we also add an additional fine-tuning layer to freeze the parameters of the pre-trained model. The input sequence representation is transformed into:

$$X = [X_1, X_2, \cdots, X_L] \tag{12}$$

where L is the length of the sequence. Finally, we map the final sequence to a linear space through the feedforward neural network for autoregressive text generation.

$$p_j = softmax\,(W^e X_j + b^e) \tag{13}$$

where X_j represents the j-th word of X, and j is in the range of $[1, L]$. The vector p_j is the probability distribution based on a autoregressive masking mechanism.

$$e_{(u,i)} = \arg\max \sum_{j}^{L} \log p_{j+c} \tag{14}$$

where $e_{(u,i)}$ represents the final explanation based on the interactions of user u and item i, and c is the length of the soft prompt.

For each user-item pair in the training set, we employ the negative log-likelihood loss (NLL) as the objective function. The loss function is defined as follows:

$$L_e = \frac{1}{\Omega} \sum_{u,i \in \Omega} \frac{1}{|G_{(u,i)}|} \sum_{j=1}^{|G_{(u,i)}|} - \log p_{j+3} \tag{15}$$

where $|G_{(u,i)}|$ denotes the length of input review texts after preprocessing, and the probability p_j is offset by three positions.

3.4 Joint Training Algorithm

The goal of joint training is to simultaneously integrate the rating prediction and explanation generation tasks into a multi-task learning framework, enhancing recommendation performance while generating personalized explanations. We define the objective function as follows:

$$L = \min\left(\lambda_r L_r + \lambda_e L_e + \lambda_\theta ||\theta||^2\right) \tag{16}$$

where L_r and L_e respectively represent the losses on the rating prediction task and the explanation generation task, θ is the set of parameters, and λ_θ denotes the regularization coefficient. The primary process of this model is shown in Fig. 2.

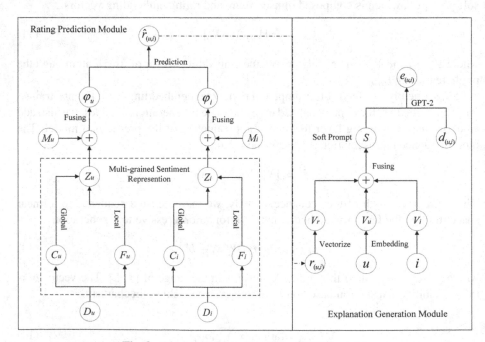

Fig. 2. Graphical illustration of our SAPER model

4 Experiments

4.1 Datasets and Experimental Settings

To demonstrate the effectiveness of our proposed model, we conduct experimental evaluations on three public datasets from recommendation applications. The three datasets cover various domains, including TripAdvisor[1] (hotel), Amazon Clothing (clothing) and Amazon Movies[2] (movies and TV). Now we have listed the descriptive statistics of three datasets in Table 2.

Table 2. Statistics of experimental datasets.

Dataset	Users	Items	Reviews
TripAdvisor	9765	6280	320023
Amazon Clothing	38764	22919	179223
Amazon Movies	7506	7360	441783

4.2 Evaluation Metrics

For the rating prediction task, we use RMSE and MAE as evaluation criteria, which are widely used metrics for evaluating recommendation performance. Smaller values of RMSE and MAE indicate that the predicted ratings are closer to the ground-truth ratings, signifying higher recommendation accuracy.

For the explanation generation task, we employ the following metrics to assess the quality of generated texts: BLEU-1, BLEU-4, and recall of ROUGE-1, ROUGE-2 and ROUGE-L. These metrics are calculated based on the content overlap between the generated explanation text and the real reviews. Larger values of BLEU and ROUGE mean higher quality generated explanations.

4.3 Baselines

To evaluate our model performance, we conduct comparative experiments with the following state-of-the-art baselines:

- SVD++ [23] decomposes the user-item rating matrix to map users and items into a latent feature space based on matrix factorization.
- NRT [16] is the first model to simultaneously perform rating prediction and explanation generation. This model uses MLP to encode users and items into vector representations, and then generates abstract tips through GRU.
- Att2Seq [17] adopts the deep neural network to jointly model users and items, and generates explanatory text through two layers of LSTM.

---

[1] https://www.tripadvisor.com
[2] http://jmcauley.ucsd.edu/data/amazon

- PETER [20] by designing a personalized Transformer, effectively unifying the two major tasks of rating prediction and explanation generation.
- PEPLER [21] focuses on efficiently integrating user and item IDs into the GPT-2 model to enhance the interpretability of recommendation systems.

4.4 Performance Comparisons

Table 3 shows the experimental results in explanation generation task. We summarize the following observations:

- Our SAPER has a significant advantage in the explanation generation task. Compare to the baselines, SAPER exhibits an average improvement by 9.41% in BLEU-1, 18.73% BLEU-4, 10.18% in ROUGE-1, 25.00% in ROUGE-2 and 10.35% in ROUGE-L on three datasets. This demonstrates the advantage of joint training for review-based recommendation, and also validates the effectiveness of introducing soft prompts strategy for explanation texts generation.
- We can see that methods based on pre-trained models (SAPER, PEPLER) outperform other shallow neural models (NRT, Att2Seq, PETER). The experimental results demonstrate the potent capabilities of the pre-trained model in natural language generation tasks.
- As a multi-task recommendation algorithm, it can be seen that SAPER outperforms NRT and PETER on all datasets. This also illustrates the effectiveness of soft prompts strategy which simultaneously corporates static features and rating-level information.

Table 3. Experimental results of explanation generation task.

Datasets	Metrics	NRT	Att2Seq	PETER	PEPLER	SAPER	Impro%
TripAdvisor	BLEU-1	15.37	15.36	15.93	16.04	**16.18**	3.26
	BLEU-4	1.01	1.00	1.07	1.11	**1.11**	6.16
	ROUGE-1	15.40	15.63	16.06	16.19	**17.38**	9.91
	ROUGE-2	1.99	1.93	2.04	2.21	**2.63**	29.09
	ROUGE-L	14.10	14.06	14.64	14.76	**16.12**	12.08
Amazon Clothing	BLEU-1	11.37	10.38	13.31	13.87	**13.94**	15.53
	BLEU-4	0.66	0.72	0.88	1.02	**1.02**	28.03
	ROUGE-1	12.17	11.72	14.49	15.01	**15.07**	14.20
	ROUGE-2	1.30	1.49	1.86	1.99	**2.08**	28.99
	ROUGE-L	10.90	10.54	12.69	13.19	**13.35**	13.89
Amazon Movies	BLEU-1	12.58	12.96	13.15	13.66	**14.31**	9.44
	BLEU-4	0.86	0.90	0.95	1.09	**1.15**	22.01

(continued)

Table 3. (*continued*)

Datasets	Metrics	NRT	Att2Seq	PETER	PEPLER	SAPER	Impro%
	ROUGE-1	14.19	13.94	14.07	14.48	**15.08**	6.44
	ROUGE-2	1.73	1.67	1.79	1.95	**2.08**	16.91
	ROUGE-L	12.91	12.95	12.64	12.90	**13.50**	5.07

Table 4 shows the experimental result in rating prediction task. We can observe that the model which considers both rating data and review texts (NRT, PETER, SAPER) outperforms the model which only considers rating data (SVD++). This is because review text contains a wealth of semantic information, and it can complement the rating data in a significant way. In addition, for the rating prediction task, the performance of SAPER does not show a significant improvement. The possible reason is that our work was centered around the explanation generation task. During the joint training process, we redefined the weight coefficients of the objective function as 1:10, which may result in less performance improvement to rating prediction.

Table 4. Experimental results of rating prediction task.

Model	TripAdvisor		Amazon Clothing		Amazon Movies	
	RMSE	MAE	RMSE	MAE	RMSE	MAE
SVD++	0.8037	0.6148	1.0646	0.8532	0.9560	0.7156
NRT	**0.7949**	0.6143	1.0535	0.8451	0.9536	0.7119
PETER	0.8104	0.6285	1.0621	0.8510	0.9524	0.7155
SAPER	0.7951	**0.6141**	**1.0529**	**0.8402**	**0.9509**	**0.7114**

5 Discussions

To further validate the performance of our model, we conducted a series of experiments on three datasets for explainable recommendation analysis. This study designed multiple model variants in terms of soft prompt text, multi-granularity sentiment fusion and parameter sensitivity analysis.

5.1 Effectiveness of Soft Prompt Text

The soft prompt text includes user vectors V_u, item vectors V_i, and corresponding rating embedding V_r. To evaluate the effectiveness of different prompt information on the explanation generation task, we conducted comparative experiments with unprompted text (Disable-prompt) and only considering user and item information (Disable-rating) on three datasets. The results are shown in Fig. 3.

It can be observed as follows: First, compared to SAPER, the performance of Disable-prompt that lacks prompt information significantly declines. This is because the pre-trained model is unable to learn the user and item features when just inputting the review texts, thus resulting in generated explainable texts that lack personalization. Second, our SAPER model performs better than the Disable-rating model that only considers user and item information. The results indicate that during the prompt stage, incorporating rating-level information can influence the semantics of soft prompts, further validating the effectiveness of our model strategy. Therefore, selecting appropriate soft prompt text is the key to achieving better performance in prompt learning.

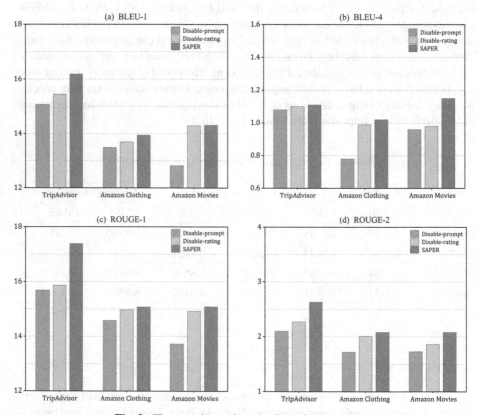

Fig. 3. The experimental results for soft prompt text

5.2   Effectiveness of Multi-granularity Sentiment Fusion

To explore the effectiveness of multi-granularity sentiment analysis on review texts, we designed two variations of models for comparative experiments: removing the global feature extraction module (Disable-global), and removing the local feature extraction module (Disable-local). The experimental results are shown in Fig. 4. We can observe that the recommendation performance of our SAPER model is better than other comparative models. This indicates that by jointly modeling review texts and integrating sentiment at both coarse-grained and fine-grained levels, it can help to obtain a more comprehensive and accurate understanding of user preferences, and fully demonstrates the effectiveness of the multi-granularity sentiment fusion strategy.

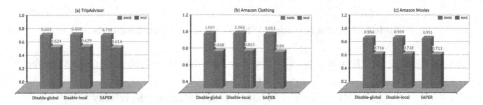

Fig. 4. The experimental results for sentiment analysis task

5.3 Parameter Sensitivity Analysis

The model utilizes the balance coefficient in the loss function to control the weight of rating prediction and explanation generation. This helps the model strike a balance between the two learning tasks. The experiments assume that λ_e is equals to 1, and the results on Amazon Clothing dataset are shown in Fig. 5. It can be observed that as λ_r increases, the performance of the explanation recommendation model first improves and then declines, reaching its peak when λ_r equals 0.1. This indicates that selecting a balance coefficient can enhance the training performance of the model, and improve its interpretability in the explanation recommendation task.

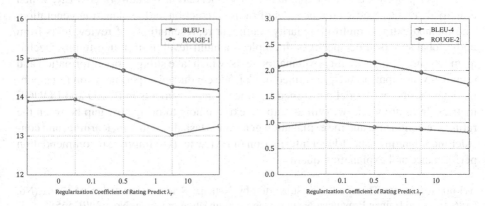

Fig. 5. The experimental results on Amazon Clothing with varying λ_r

5.4 Case Study

To validate the quality of generated explanation texts, we conducted a case study on three baselines. From Table 5, it can be seen that the explanation texts generated by

SAPER are more expressive and closer to the real reviews. The proposed method uses a pretrained model with powerful language modeling capabilities, which is trained based on a large corpus of data, resulting in higher quality and readability of the generated texts. Additionally, by extracting multi-granularity sentiment from reviews, SAPER are helpful for capturing user sentiment preferences and interpretability.

Table 5. Generate explainable texts of several selected methods.

Amazon Clothing	Real Review	They are the most comfortable shoes I own and feel great
	NRT	I have a wide foot and it fits perfectly
	PEPLER	I have a very high instep and these fit me well
	SAPER	I love the shirt **fits great** and the material is very **comfortable**
Amazon Movies	Real Review	It's a great film that looks so beautiful on this DVD
	NRT	This movie is a great movie
	PEPLER	The colors are vibrant and the music is beautiful
	SAPER	The animation is **beautiful** and the story is **well told**

6 Conclusions

This paper proposes a novel explainable recommendation framework SAPER, which effectively unifies the two major tasks of rating prediction and explanation generation. The method extracts multi-granularity sentiment representations of review texts from both global and local perspectives. It employs a multi-level prompt fine-tuning mechanism to generate high-quality explanation texts, which take soft prompt information and review text as inputs to the pre-trained model. We conducted experiments on three public datasets, and our model performed significant improvements in BLEU and ROUGE metrics. In future work, we will attempt to explore how to bridge the gap between the rating prediction task and the explanation generation task through joint learning, and consider incorporating aspect-level information of review texts to improve recommendation performance and explanation quality.

Acknowledgment. This work was supported by National Science Foundation of China (No. 61862021) and Hainan Provincial Natural Science Foundation of China (No. 620RC565).

References

1. Tay, Y., Luu, A.T., Hui, S.C.: Multi-pointer co-attention networks for recommendation. In: Proceedings of the 24th ACM SIGKDD International Conference on Knowledge Discovery & Data Mining, pp. 2309–2318 (2018)

2. Koren, Y., Bell, R., Volinsky, C.: Matrix factorization techniques for recommender systems. Computer **42**, 30–37 (2009)
3. Tang, X., Hao, B., Dang, X., Zhong, B., Wang, R., Yan, Z.: Text semantic understanding based on knowledge enhancement and multi-granular feature extraction. In: 2020 Chinese Automation Congress (CAC), pp. 337–341. IEEE (2020)
4. Hada, D.V., Shevade, S.K.: ReXPlug: explainable recommendation using plug-and-play language model. In: Proceedings of the 44th International ACM SIGIR Conference on Research and Development in Information Retrieval, pp. 81–91 (2021)
5. McAuley, J., Leskovec, J.: Hidden factors and hidden topics: understanding rating dimensions with review text. In: Proceedings of the 7th ACM Conference on Recommender Systems, pp. 165–172. Association for Computing Machinery, Hong Kong, China (2013)
6. Wang, C., Blei, D.M.: Collaborative topic modeling for recommending scientific articles. In: Proceedings of the 17th ACM SIGKDD International Conference on Knowledge Discovery and Data Mining, pp. 448–456. Association for Computing Machinery, San Diego, California, USA (2011)
7. Kim, D., Park, C., Oh, J., Lee, S., Yu, H.: Convolutional matrix factorization for document context-aware recommendation. In: Proceedings of the 10th ACM Conference on Recommender Systems, pp. 233–240. Association for Computing Machinery, Boston, Massachusetts, USA (2016)
8. Zheng, L., Noroozi, V., Yu, P.S.: Joint deep modeling of users and items using reviews for recommendation. In: Proceedings of the Tenth ACM International Conference on Web Search and Data Mining, pp. 425–434. Association for Computing Machinery, Cambridge, United Kingdom (2017)
9. Chen, C., Zhang, M., Liu, Y., Ma, S.: Neural attentional rating regression with review-level explanations. In: Proceedings of the 2018 World Wide Web Conference, pp. 1583–1592. International World Wide Web Conferences Steering Committee, Lyon, France (2018)
10. Pham, D.-H., Le, A.-C., Le, T.-K.-C.: Learning word embeddings for aspect-based sentiment analysis. In: Hasida, K., Pa, W. (eds.) Computational Linguistics: 15th International Conference of the Pacific Association for Computational Linguistics, PACLING 2017, Yangon, Myanmar, 16–18 August 2017, Revised Selected Papers, vol. 15, pp. 28–40. Springer, Cham (2018). https://doi.org/10.1007/978-981-10-8438-6_3
11. Hoang, M., Bihorac, O.A., Rouces, J.: Aspect-based sentiment analysis using BERT. In: Proceedings of the 22nd Nordic Conference on Computational Linguistics, pp. 187–196 (2019)
12. Yang, C., Chen, X., Liu, L., Sweetser, P.: Leveraging semantic features for recommendation: sentence-level emotion analysis. Inf. Process. Manage. **58**, 102543 (2021)
13. Cai, Y., Ke, W., Cui, E., Yu, F.: A deep recommendation model of cross-grained sentiments of user reviews and ratings. Inf. Process. Manage. **59**, 102842 (2022)
14. Seo, S., Huang, J., Yang, H., Liu, Y.: Interpretable convolutional neural networks with dual local and global attention for review rating prediction. In: Proceedings of the Eleventh ACM Conference on Recommender Systems, pp. 297–305. Association for Computing Machinery, Como, Italy (2017)
15. Wu, L., Quan, C., Li, C., Wang, Q., Zheng, B., Luo, X.: A Context-aware user-item representation learning for item recommendation. ACM Trans. Inf. Syst. **37**, 1–29 (2019)
16. Li, P., Wang, Z., Ren, Z., Bing, L., Lam, W.: Neural rating regression with abstractive tips generation for recommendation. In: Proceedings of the 40th International ACM SIGIR Conference on Research and Development in Information Retrieval, pp. 345–354. Association for Computing Machinery, Shinjuku, Tokyo, Japan (2017)

17. Dong, L., Huang, S., Wei, F., Lapata, M., Xu, K.: Learning to generate product reviews from attributes. In: Proceedings of the 15th Conference of the European Chapter of the Association for Computational Linguistics, pp. 623–632. Association for Computational Linguistics (2017)
18. Li, P., Wang, Y., Chi, E.H., Chen, M.: Prompt tuning large language models on personalized aspect extraction for recommendations. arXiv preprint arXiv:2306.01475 (2023)
19. Han, M., Jin, T., Lin, W., Li, C., Qiao, L.: Generating questions via unexploited OCR texts: prompt-based data augmentation for TextVQA. In: 2023 International Joint Conference on Neural Networks (IJCNN), pp. 01–08. IEEE (2023)
20. Li, L., Zhang, Y., Chen, L.: Personalized transformer for explainable recommendation. In Proceedings of the 59th Annual Meeting of the Association for Computational Linguistics, pp. 4947–4957 (2021)
21. Li, L., Zhang, Y., Chen, L.: Personalized prompt learning for explainable recommendation. ACM Trans. Inf. Syst. **41**, 1–26 (2023)
22. Geng, S., Liu, S., Fu, Z., Ge, Y., Zhang, Y.: Recommendation as Language Processing (RLP): a unified Pretrain, Personalized Prompt & Predict Paradigm (P5). In: Proceedings of the 16th ACM Conference on Recommender Systems, pp. 299–315. Association for Computing Machinery, Seattle, WA, USA (2022)
23. Koren, Y.: Factorization meets the neighborhood: a multifaceted collaborative filtering model. In: Proceedings of the 14th ACM SIGKDD International Conference on Knowledge Discovery and Data Mining, pp. 426–434 (2008)

Author Index

F
Feng, Ziquan 47

H
He, Sheng 89

J
Jin, Mingzhe 3
Jin, Ting 116

K
Kang, Jiahao 19

L
Li, Jiayun 60
Li, Wentao 60
Liang, Bin 34
Lin, Hongfei 19
Lin, Hongquan 89
Lin, Qihui 34
Lin, Yuan 19
Liu, Dachang 75
Long, Xiuhua 116
Lou, Chenwei 34
Lu, Yong 3, 47, 60
Luo, Cheng 75
Lv, Haifeng 89

M
Mao, Ruibin 34, 75

N
Ning, Ke 89
Ning, Yishuang 89

S
Sun, Na 47
Sun, Wenyi 75
Sun, Yuefan 19

W
Wang, Depei 75
Wang, Qianlong 34
Wang, Zhenxi 3
Wen, Zhiyuan 34

X
Xie, Weipeng 100
Xu, Ruifeng 34, 75

Y
Yang, Liang 19
Yi, Chao 60

Z
Zhang, Jianxian 100
Zhang, Shaowu 19
Zhang, Wenyan 100
Zhao, Lifeng 47
Zheng, Xianghan 100

Printed in the United States
by Baker & Taylor Publisher Services

Printed in the United States
by Baker & Taylor Publisher Services